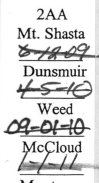

THE WALL STREET JOURNAL GUIDE TO

The End of Wall Street As We Know It

THE WALL STREET JOURNAL GUIDE TO

The End of Wall Street As We Know It

What You Need to Know About

the Greatest Financial Crisis of Our Time—

and How to Survive It

DAVE KANSAS

COLLINS BUSINESS

An Imprint of HarperCollins Publishers

This book is written as a source of information only, and the information contained in it should not be considered a substitute for the advice, decisions or judgment of the reader's professional advisors. Each investor's situation is different, and readers are encouraged to seek professional advice before making any investment decisions.

Illustrations on pages 15, 77, 98, 99, and 167 are used courtesy of *The Wall Street Journal*.

FIRST EDITION

Designed by Jaime Putorti

Library of Congress Cataloging-in-Publication Data is available upon request.

ISBN-13: 978-0-06-1788406

09 10 11 12 13 DIX/RRD 10 9 8 7 6 5 4 3 2 1

To Monica, my lovely wife

CONTENTS

Contents

Contents

Contents

Contents

INTRODUCTION

I N THE PAST YEAR, both the U.S. and global financial systems have changed so radically that few, if any, could have predicted it. Large banks have failed, Wall Street's investment banks have essentially become extinct and borrowing has become exceedingly difficult for both companies and individuals. In order to try to save the financial system and boost the flagging economy, the government has extended more than $7 trillion—about half the total annual U.S. economic output—in various guarantees and loans.

In December, the National Bureau of Economic Research declared that the U.S. economy had officially fallen into recession at the end of 2007. Since then, tens of thousands of home foreclosures, millions of lost jobs and withered investment and retirement portfolios have added to a grim picture. It is an economic firestorm with little precedent, and its solutions will take some time to work out. Over the course of the chaos, not only have banks and companies "too big to fail" collapsed, but, in the case of Iceland, an entire nation is grappling with insolvency. Worldwide bank runs, once considered a throwback to financial panics past, grabbed headlines, and Main Street individuals feared for the safety of their cash deposits built up over a lifetime of work.

At the same time, stock markets around the globe fell sharply, surprising and angering many people who had counted on their portfolios for retirement and college payments for their children. The sharp drop in share prices forced recent retirees back to work, and those close to retiring began considering years more of work to put their broken nest eggs back together again. We're experiencing a moment when nothing and no one feels safe. In the wake of the $50-billion Bernard Madoff scandal, charities and even the very rich found themselves facing huge losses.

People are understandably frustrated and angry. Billions of dollars go to bail out banks, while families try to figure out how to make ends meet in straitened times. Fears of more lost jobs ripple through the country. It is a time of high anxiety with moments of panic arguably not seen in this nation since the Great Depression, even if the present circumstances don't exactly mirror the calamity of that age. Despite the horrible economic environment, vast shantytowns have not sprung up around major cities, and the unemployment rate, though higher than in the recent past, is still miles from the 25% seen in the 1930s.

How did this happen? In simple terms, everyone—banks, companies and individuals—borrowed far too much money and invested that money unwisely. Individuals bought more real estate than they could afford. Banks invested in mortgage-related debt that crumpled in value. Some banks borrowed as much as $35 for every $1 they invested, meaning that when things went bad, they went bad in a hurry.

All financial crises throughout time have boiled down to greed and overconfidence. From the Dutch tulip madness in the 1600s to the insanity surrounding outrageously valued Internet stocks in the more recent past, greed has driven irrational behavior, which always ends with the true value of pumped-up prices coming to light. In this case, greed drove unreasonable real estate purchases. Greed led banks to lend more money than they could reasonably expect to recoup. Greed inspired people throughout the financial system to do illogical things in the hope of ultimately getting rich.

Overconfidence meant that caution—on the part of investors, borrowers and lenders of all stripes—evaporated. Overconfidence meant that risk-management standards at even the most venerable financial institutions fell by the wayside. Overconfidence meant that too few planned for anything to go wrong. The combination of greed and overconfidence led to a financial hurricane that swept all of us before it.

Though the recent events have left people gobsmacked, the truth is, we've experienced financial panics before, though rarely of the scope and magnitude of the one we're living through today. Those of us who lived through the 1970s remember a period of high inflation and lackluster economic growth. Malaise during that period reached such a level that many wondered if the economy would ever recover. Of course, the economy recovered spectacularly in the 1980s after a tough recession in the early part of that decade.

As a financial journalist, I've witnessed other financial panics. The Asian financial crisis of 1997. The Russian crisis of 1998. The bursting of the Internet and technology stock bubble in 2000–2001. But all of these lacked the comprehensive nature of the financial crisis of 2007–2008. The notion that the "center might not hold"—that the entire system of liberal capitalism might fail—almost never became a topic of discussion during these earlier crises. But this time, the crisis took on these kinds of existential terms.

I've written about the financial markets in both good times and bad. As a reporter at *The Wall Street Journal* in 1995, I wrote about the Dow Jones Industrial Average bursting through 5,000. That sure feels like a long time ago. As editor in chief of TheStreet.com, I had a ringside seat to the crazy run-up of Internet stocks in the late 1990s. And during the early part of this century, I oversaw coverage of Wall Street for *The Wall Street Journal* during a time of rising markets.

It was during that last stint that the seeds of our present problems were sown. My colleagues and I wrote frequently about the overabundance of "easy money." It seemed that any hedge fund could borrow buckets of money from overeager banks with few restrictions. Individuals with modest means could take out a mortgage to buy a house well beyond their wildest dreams or, tragically, their basic means. Savvy Wall Street wizards created exotic investment instruments to take advantage of the oceans of debt flowing into the system. From the outside, it looked like a crazy merry-go-round that could keep going as long as the music never stopped.

But, of course, the music did stop. And all that debt turned out to have driven investment choices that ultimately made little sense. Enormous losses swamped banks, individuals and the entire system. Even as you read this, the great sorting out is continuing. Sometimes, such periods can take a long time. The Dow Jones Industrial Average didn't reach its 1929 peak again until 1954. Other times, recovery from a nightmare can come quite quickly. The 1987 stock market crash—when the Dow Jones industrials fell 22% in a single October day—hardly made a dent in the economy. And the Dow recovered its losses in less than a year.

What can we expect in the coming years? First we need to know better what has happened. From experienced bankers to neophyte homeowners, the travails of the past two years remain somewhat of a mystery. This book will explain the origins and events of the financial crisis. It will then give you guidance on how best to cope with its aftermath. It is a combination of history and strategic insight for these new times.

THE WALL STREET JOURNAL GUIDE TO

The End of
Wall Street
As We Know It

ONE

"MORE RISK IS SIMPLY MORE PROFIT"

IT GOES WITHOUT SAYING that risk is at the heart of a capitalist system. The worrying, the chin scratching, nail-biting and hair pulling that go with it are part and parcel of an economy organized around risk. You can take a calculated risk, a measured risk or an educated risk. But you can't eliminate risk from capitalism without turning it into a system more akin to socialism or communism. You can't have capitalism without some level of risk. And you can't have risk without some level of worry. In the current environment, sometimes the level of worry has exceeded logic. In early December, for instance, short-term Treasury notes actually traded with a negative yield. That meant investors were paying the government to lend it money, an exceedingly rare quirk that underscored the high degrees of fear and worry in the marketplace.

During the twenty years prior to our current financial crisis, concerns about risk steadily diminished. The recovery from the 1987 crash came so quickly that investors embraced the philosophy of "buying on the dips." The notion: stocks eventually recover, so buying on declines made eminent sense. This, however, is a fairly flabby notion. Not every drop recovers so quickly. Buyers of Japanese stocks during the "dip" of the early 1990s are still waiting for a recovery. The same goes for those who bought a number of Internet stocks after they fell from great heights to near oblivion.

In the 1990s, the savings-and-loan fiasco seemed enormous at first. Savings & Loans, sometimes known as thrifts, had lent large amounts of money to developers with grandiose real estate plans. When those plans failed, many savings-and-loan institutions failed, property developments went bust and the government had to step in with billions of dollars to rescue the S&Ls. But the problem seemed to fade away fairly quickly once the rescue got under way with the establishment of the Resolution Trust Corp. The RTC bought up the bad stuff and eventually resold it once the market recovered. In the end, the cost of the S&L crisis, in inflation-adjusted dollars, came out to a mere $256 billion—a pale echo of the trillions in bailout money already deployed in the current crisis.

In late 1997 came the Asian financial crisis. The contagion from that crisis led to huge losses around the globe and even forced the New York Stock Exchange to close trading early during one session—something that hasn't happened in the current crisis. But the crisis had few lasting effects. The Asian economies and markets recovered briskly, and the U.S. market resumed its Internet and technology stock mania. Again, it seemed that risky events resolved themselves rapidly. The fear of risk diminished by one more notch.

Many people lost money and businesses went under when the Internet and technology bubble burst. But the economy suffered little collateral damage. Even an event as devastating as the September 11, 2001, terrorist attacks did not have a permanent impact on markets. Manhattan real estate prices momentarily buckled, but by December of that same year, prices started shooting higher, even as the World Trade Center site smoldered.

For nearly two decades, it seemed as though nothing much could shake the confidence of global markets. Recessions were getting shorter and milder, expansions becoming longer. Developing giants such as China, India and Brazil fed global economic growth. A peso crisis, Russian and Argentine debt defaults, wars, famines and uprisings came and went as the markets and global economies steamrollered ahead.

As the 2000s began, confidence in the resiliency of the financial system couldn't have been higher and conversations with Wall Street professionals couldn't have been more surreal. In 2004, I asked the head of a major European bank about the widespread notion that his bank behaved more like a hedge fund, making large bets with both its own money and borrowed money, This risk-taking often centered on speculative market bets or investments in exotic financial instruments, often referred to as derivatives. "Aren't you concerned about taking on so much risk?" His response: "More risk is simply more profit."

A short time later, a Wall Street executive, when asked a similar question about how his firm felt comfortable using large amounts of its own capital to make risky market investments and fund acquisitions that required large amounts of debt, said, "We have learned to master the distribution and management of risk." Wall Street firms, including Morgan Stanley, Goldman Sachs and Bear Stearns insisted that they had "stress tested" their systems and figured out how to minimize exposure. They said they were prepared for the 100-year storm, should it come. Of course, this was just talk. Few people really expected such a storm to come. Indeed, as financial instruments became more complicated, the risk-management systems couldn't keep up with the transactions, thus undercutting the efficacy of the so-called system stress testing. The reported "value at risk," a measure of the danger Wall Street firms faced in crisis, gave a false sense of security and order to a marketplace increasingly based on frightening levels of risk.

VALUE AT RISK

Value at risk (VAR) was a wonderfully complex mathematical model that provided Wall Street firms with a way to communicate to investors and regulators how much risk exposure they had. At its simplest, VAR indicates how much money a firm stands to lose in a sharp market movement. The concept was developed through academic work and became a popular measure in the late 1980s in the wake of the 1987 stock market crash—a day when stocks fell 22% in a single session. Since then, VAR has evolved and taken on a more public role as investment firms cite the measure to assure investors that they are paying careful attention to their risk profile.

Wall Street firms dutifully report their VAR in their quarterly financial statements. And though the number rose ahead of the financial whirlwind, the increase failed to rattle those running the firms. Indeed, going by VAR measures, it's hard to believe that Lehman Brothers, Bear Stearns and Merrill Lynch didn't survive.

Critics charge that VAR is too general a measure of risk to be effective. For instance, VAR may not capture all the risks in the marketplace adequately. Academics who have worked on risk modeling often find that unanticipated events, called "Black Swans" by VAR critic and author Nassim Taleb, simply can't be accounted for properly, undercutting the efficacy of VAR figures. Moreover, VAR conveys a sense of adept risk management that might not be warranted, primarily because of the inability to anticipate so-called Black Swan events. When Wall Street firms began amping up their borrowing to boost their investments, they would point to their VAR to explain that they had everything well in hand. Alas.

It's clear that such risk-management strategies failed for most Wall Street firms. VAR is one tool of many, but over-reliance on VAR measures helped feed the confidence that builds to illogical levels ahead of a financial panic.

Although some commentators identified the housing market as the likely source of future problems, many other market experts found themselves looking in all the wrong places for a possible systemic collapse in the system. The hunt for "the big one"—the trigger that would lead to systemic crisis—almost invariably focused on the dollar. In April 2006, Paul Krugman, Nobel Prize winner in Economics in 2008 and columnist for the *New York Times*, wrote a paper titled: "Will There Be a Dollar Crisis." In that paper, he outlined the intense academic debate surrounding the dollar's fate and noted that several of his colleagues inside and outside academia feared a potential dollar-driven economic crisis. Outside of academia, market strategists frequently opined that the U.S., with its huge borrowings, stood vulnerable to a deep drop in the value of the dollar. Economist Stephen Roach at Morgan Stanley saw the anemic, bedraggled currency as ripe for a long decline. America's staggering deficits, ill-disciplined government spending and profligate consumerism meant that the dollar lived more on reputation than on reality. "The big one" would come with a huge run on the dollar, leading to systemic market failure that would introduce a global recession and a lower standard of living for all Americans.

This scenario may happen some day, but it is not the tsunami that actually struck. As long as the U.S. faces heavy deficits, both fiscal and in its global trade balance, the dollar remains vulnerable to a sharp decline. Such a decline would certainly aggravate the present crisis, but experts are split on whether such a drop would lead to intense economic difficulty or merely be embarrassing and politically enfeebling to the U.S. But for the present, fears about a dollar crisis don't seem a large concern. Indeed, the value of the dollar has actually risen against major currencies during the financial crisis. The dollar doomsters overlooked several key points when making their case. First (and really first, second, third and fourth), China needs the U.S. to grow, because the U.S. buys its stuff. Through September 2008, the U.S. had a negative trade balance with China of $195 billion. Without such robust purchases of Chinese goods, the hundreds of millions of very poor Chinese will remain very poor for a very long time, creating a political climate the Chinese leaders don't want. Someday the Chinese may have a healthy and broad enough economy and be solvent enough to no longer feel a need to buy dollars in order to help the U.S. purchase its goods to support its own economy. But until that day, if it comes, they will keep accumulating dollars.

Second, as troubled as the U.S. economy is, few nations are in much better financial shape. The countries of the European Union are saddled with their own debt and deficit problems. In 2008, Britain had a total debt of 42% of GDP, above the government target of 40%, and its fiscal deficit was on the rise. France had a projected budget deficit of 3% of GDP in 2008, which is higher than the participants in the euro currency are supposed to carry. Nor is Asia immune. Japan's fiscal deficit is relatively small, but it has a total debt burden of more than 140% of its GDP—the biggest such burden in the world. Though not exactly the best argument for a nation's strength, the case that the U.S. is "not as bad" as everyone else still resonates in global markets.

Third, the dollar remains the chief global reserve currency.

The young euro (about a decade old) is also important, but at the end of the day, nearly all countries hold the dollar as their principal reserve currency. If the dollar were to go bust, economies the world over would suffer terribly, an occurrence they would naturally prefer not to happen.

So the dollar doom scenario has powerful points against it—which might explain why it wasn't the trigger of our financial troubles. Instead, as has been the case nearly every time, the storm came from unexpected places—the collapse in the housing market and the vast debt and complex investments arrayed around that market—and wrought unexpectedly massive damage. The costs of the calamity are still being calculated today. Already huge companies, such as Bear Stearns, Lehman Brothers, Washington Mutual and Wachovia have failed or been consumed by other institutions. More than a million people have lost their jobs, and taxpayers will bear the burden, directly and indirectly, of the more than $7 trillion of loans, guarantees and bailout funds for years to come.

In the end, the financial storm came because the system no longer feared risk. Instead, it saw risk as a one-way opportunity. More risk, more reward. Piling on billions of dollars in borrowed money, the entire system moved in a single direction, gobbling up risk and setting the stage for a dramatic collapse that would bring fear back to the marketplace in a way not seen in decades. As it turned out, more risk meant more disaster.

We've Figured It Out

"This time, it's different."

This phrase sparks fear and trembling on Wall Street as no other. It causes otherwise rational people to throw judgment, experience and caution to the wind. When tech stocks zoomed amid the New Economy excitement, cheerleaders declared this a new, different era—and in some ways it was. The New Economy and its new technology—email, PDAs, social networking—have certainly entrenched themselves in our everyday life, but, as too many of us learned the hard way, the investment promise of this incredible new era crashed and burned in 2000.

Of course, it was hardly the first time Wall Street fell prey to the lure of so-called certainty. Two decades before the dot-com boom, investors believed that big, blue-chip companies such as Procter & Gamble, Coca-Cola and Dow Chemical Co. ("the Nifty Fifty") would dominate the global economy forevermore. The Nifty Fifty rose dramatically only to come crashing down to earth as more rational growth expectations took hold. Of course, many of the Nifty Fifty, such as P&G, remain solid bets. But others—Polaroid, for instance—are barely shadows of their former selves.

These market "mistakes"—the demise of the dot-com boom and the end of the Nifty Fifty—pale in comparison to what we're going through today. Though many people lost money, some quite a lot of money, in the dot-com bust, the bust did not threaten the broader financial system. The government for the most part could sit by and watch it happen. Indeed, regulators and professional investors were far more scared when the hedge fund Long-Term Capital Management imploded in 1998 in the midst of the Internet boom.

In retrospect, the implosion of Long-Term Capital Management can be seen as a red flag signaling that global markets were more fragile than anyone believed. In fact, its collapse bore many of the hallmarks of the subprime crisis and credit crunch that would come ten years later.

In order to combat the crisis stemming from LTCM's collapse, the Federal Reserve dropped short-term interest rates in emergency fashion. It then gathered the heads of the Wall Street and national banking firms in a single room to hammer out a solution to save LTCM and, by extension, the financial system itself. How could this little-known hedge fund have put the entire economy in danger?

First, in a scenario that should now sound quite familiar, LTCM borrowed a ton of money from banks, investment banks and other financial institutions to make its investment bets. In some circumstances, it borrowed more than $30 for every $1 invested, something that many of the firms that ran into deep trouble during the current financial crisis did as well. If you're onto a good investing strategy, borrowed money will amplify your gains. If, however, your bets are going wrong, borrowed money will amplify your problems like kerosene on an unwanted fire. In the current crisis, enormous amounts of borrowed money, eagerly supplied by financial institutions, helped magnify the problems that initially stemmed from a declining real estate market.

Second, LTCM used complicated quantitative investment models—and believed in them. These models, used primarily in the construction of convoluted investment instruments, also played a key role in the present financial crisis. And confidence in this modeling led many banks to make bad decisions because faith in the modeling was so strong. Similarly, LTCM kept driving bets because it had computational "certainty" that eventually its bets would turn out right. LTCM even had economics Nobel laureates Myron Scholes and Robert C. Merton on the team, giving them even more quantitative confidence. So, like a blackjack player chasing losses, they kept betting and betting and betting, knowing that certainty was on their side.

But, of course, it wasn't. Instead, by the time LTCM couldn't shake its pockets for another nickel to bet, its enormous borrowing, often called leverage in investing circles, and its heavy use of complex instruments had placed it dangerously in the middle of the global financial highway. Its failure would ripple throughout the system with untold impact. Regulators feared the worst. That's why regulators, led by the Federal Reserve, worked quickly to hammer out a rescue of LTCM. The rescue essentially required Wall Street banks to provide more than $3 billion in financing to save LTCM. The alternative to that rescue—a seizing up of credit markets—looked worse. Such a rescue mentality, driven by similar motivations, would resurface during the financial crisis of 2007–2008, but in a much larger way.

Not long after that rescue, the markets resumed their march higher. Outlandish enthusiasm accompanied the dot-com boom, and investors grew fabulously rich betting on companies they didn't understand. LTCM? Forgotten nearly as quickly as it had arrived on the scene.

In retrospect, LTCM provided a stark foreshadowing of trouble up ahead. How had the fund been able to borrow so much so easily? How could a single hedge fund, and not a particularly large one at that, have created such widespread fear and panic? Was the system so fragile? As the party rolled on in dot-com land, some people grappled with these concerns. But, for the most part, LTCM fell by the wayside, forgotten as a group of overconfident geniuses and nothing more.

The market's sharp rallies in 1999 and 2000 quickly became its own investment bubble, ending with the collapse in Internet stock prices coupled with some old-fashioned scandal. Enron and Arthur Andersen disappeared, and a number of Internet and tech companies better known by their stock symbols than by anything they did or made also ceased to exist. Among the scandal-ridden casualties? WorldCom. A telecommunications company run by Bernie Ebbers, an erstwhile Sunday School teacher, had collapsed amid charges of the books being cooked. Many of its smaller competitors also imploded during this period as predictions of unlimited telecommunications demand sank along with all the dead dot-coms.

But a funny thing happened amid that collapse. No bank or investment company of note failed because of the telecom debt implosion. Historians will no doubt see this as the Dog That Didn't Bark moment of financial engineering. Few people even recall the scale of that debt collapse, mostly because it was so easily absorbed by the system.

One reason the telecom debt collapse didn't harm more participants was the growing use of a tactic we're all hearing a lot of these days: in order to spread out risk to a broader group of investors, Wall Street financial engineers developed ever more complex "derivatives." Derivatives, which I'll discuss in greater detail in the next chapter, are simply investment instruments based on an underlying security—in other words, investments derived from another security. For instance, stock options are derived from stocks but are traded at another point in time. They give buyers the right, but not the obligation, to purchase stock at a specific price on a specific future date.

But the derivatives that became popular in the last decade were and are far more complex than stock options. These derivatives, when they worked properly, helped mitigate risk. Wall Street firms also securitized, or combined, assets financed through debt and sold them in bundles as another means of mitigating risk (all the while collecting fees for this service, of course). By using derivatives and securitized assets, debt risks and other risks could be spread far and wide. At least that's how the theory went.

When many telecom companies collapsed, led by World-Com, the system of credit-default swaps (a form of so-called "insurance" which I'll also be discussing in greater detail in the next chapter) and securitization (the spreading of risk) received its first big test. And it passed with flying colors. A few small banks barked about losing money, but the system rolled merrily along with few difficulties. The financial wizards grew more confident that they could master risk, and investors grew more confident that these folks knew their game well. The LTCM crisis was widely viewed as an anomaly. Even its leader, John Meriwether, had quietly worked his way back into the hedge fund, launching a new fund in 1999.

Housing

As Wall Street basked in its risk-management confidence, the housing market began to rumble to remarkable life. In the wake of the dot-com bubble bursting, the Federal Reserve chief, Alan Greenspan, eventually took short-term interest rates down to 1%, a level not seen since the 1950s. Interest rates are lowered in times of economic stress in order to make lending and borrowing cheaper and thereby help the economy recover. Despite several recessions since the 1950s, short-term interest rates had not fallen to such a low level. Mr. Greenspan lowered rates to cushion the impact of the collapsing dot-com bubble. This effort continued in the wake of the terrorist attacks of September 11, 2001. Coincidentally, Mr. Greenspan's successor, Ben Bernanke, lowered short-term rates to nearly 0% in December 2008 to fight the current financial and economic crisis.

With interest rates so low, money flowed to investments that depend heavily on debt because low interest rates make debt more affordable and easier to come by. The investment that uses enormous amounts of debt? Housing.

ALAN GREENSPAN

Alan Greenspan has watched his once-pristine reputation come under a great deal of fire during the financial crisis. Dubbed "The Maestro" by the journalist Bob Woodward in an eponymous book, Mr. Greenspan seemed to have mastered the dark arts of central banking. He presided over a great deal of prosperity, worked with presidents of both parties and became so prominent and influential that his words could move markets sharply. He also became famous for speaking with such opacity that it became well-nigh impossible to divine what exactly he was saying.

Greenspan arrived as Federal Reserve chief just ahead of the 1987 stock market crash. He managed the situation deftly, injecting liquidity into the system and helping the market rebound swiftly. Appointed by President Ronald Reagan, Greenspan was subsequently reappointed by President Bill Clinton. He served until 2006, when Ben Bernanke succeeded him.

In 1996, Greenspan talked about "irrational exuberance" in the stock market, and stock prices fell hard in response. But even Greenspan couldn't derail what became a roaring bull market in the late 1990s. The stock gains reached such a level, especially among Internet stocks, that critics called on Greenspan to raise interest rates and "burst" the bubble in stock prices. Greenspan demurred, and stock prices raced ahead to ridiculous heights.

Eventually, the bubble did burst and the Fed slashed interest rates to a record low 1% to combat the ensuing economic downturn. Critics now say that that policy unleashed an enormous appetite for debt that found its way into the housing market. In theory, the bubble in Internet stocks simply migrated into the housing market. His detractors also say his soothing words about derivatives and his faith in the free market undercut attempts to rein in the borrowing and speculation that accompanied the housing boom.

When the housing boom blew apart, the mortgage-related derivatives market cratered, leading to the financial crisis. Greenspan ended up admitting in congressional testimony in 2008 that perhaps his faith in unfettered free markets had contained some bad assumptions. Still, it's important to note that many of Greenspan's ideas gave the Federal Reserve the tools to deal with the financial crisis. And the credibility he built for the U.S. central bank, both here and overseas, has become a vital asset as central bankers and policy makers around the globe battle the financial crisis.

He is married to the television reporter Andrea Mitchell and plays a mean game of tennis.

A traditional housing purchase requires just a 20% down payment. As we'll see, that became a downright belt-and-suspenders approach as the housing industry lost its collective mind. But let's put aside some of the crazier lending practices for a moment and realize that we're still talking about 80% of borrowed money for the purchase of a home! And homes are often the most expensive asset people will ever own.

The Fed's easy-money policy began driving a torrent of money into the housing market. By taking advantage of low interest rates, developers, speculators and individuals could buy more and more homes with the same amount of money. The rapid increase in buying started prices moving smartly higher. Developers couldn't keep up with the demand, so prices continued to jump at a remarkable rate.

Over the last 100 years, home prices have risen by an average 3% a year. By 2002 they were increasing more than 15% on average and more than 25% in certain hot markets such as southern California and coastal Florida. In the wake of the stock market's huge skid, the security of homes and home

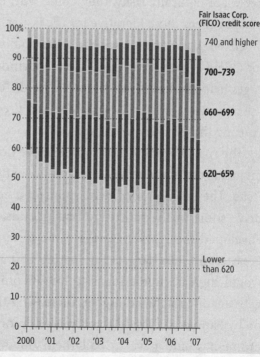

Casting a Wider Net

The surge in subprime loans included a large slice made to borrowers whose credit scores indicate that they might have qualified for loans with more favorable terms.

Percentage of subprime loans each quarter that went to borrowers within each credit-score range

Note: Data exclude non-securitized loans and those for which no data were available. Borrowers with FICO scores above 620 generally can qualify for a prime loan, though other factors could prevent that.

Source: First American Loan Performance

Fair Isaac Corp. (FICO) credit score

740 and higher

700–739

660–699

620–659

Lower than 620

values seemed like a wonderful cure. "Home prices always rise, even a little bit" became the 11th Commandment, and few doubted it.

As the housing market boomed, politicians saw an opportunity to expand the allure of home ownership among the less privileged. This coincided with a couple of other marketplace phenomena. First, those with weak or bad credit could get mortgages through something called the subprime market. "Subprime" is just a fancy way of saying that the buyer of the mortgage might not be able to pay it off. Because these mortgages are naturally risky, they come with higher interest rates, making them more lucrative for the issuer.

Given that interest rates had fallen to historic lows, the thirst for "yield"—or higher rates—was enormous. Subprime mortgages helped address that thirst for yield. To ameliorate some of the risk, two agencies, Fannie Mae and Freddie Mac, began devouring these riskier mortgages.

The role of Freddie and Fannie in the housing portion of the financial crisis mess has become an extremely controversial issue. These two government-sponsored entities clearly helped drive some of the mortgage issuance insanity that eventually enveloped the market. At the same time, lawmakers in Congress established targets for Fannie and Freddie so that they would increase home loans to low-income people. These targets steadily ratcheted higher, increasing the overall risk taken on by Fannie and Freddie and made it more likely that the government would have to bail them out in a time of trouble, which eventually happened as the financial crisis peaked.

FANNIE MAE AND FREDDIE MAC

Fannie Mae and Freddie Mac are the names of the agencies previously known as the Federal National Mortgage Association and the Federal Home Loan Mortgage Corp., two large government-backed entities that are active in the mortgage market. They own or back about half of the nation's $12 trillion mortgage market and their mandate is to help make home mortgages more affordable.

In the financial crisis of 2007–2008, Fannie and Freddie became saddled with enormous amounts of poorly performing mortgages and eventually were placed into "conservatorship" by the government, meaning that they now have the full backing of the U.S. government. Prior to the government takeover, Fannie and Freddie were so-called government-sponsored enterprises (GSEs), which had an *implied* but not an *official* backing from the government that still allowed them to secure better financing terms in the debt markets to fund their mortgage-related programs.

Other GSEs still exist, such as the Government National Mortgage Association (Ginnie Mae) and the Federal Agricultural Mortgage Corp. (Farmer Mac), but Fannie and Freddie were by far the biggest such enterprises.

Fannie Mae, founded in 1938 by the government in order to help support the mortgage markets, doesn't originate mortgages but instead purchases, trades and securitizes them in order to provide liquidity to the mortgage market. In theory, this activity helps make funds available to the banks that originate mortgages. In 1968, Fannie Mae became a government-sponsored enterprise and its shares began trading, making it a public company as opposed to a government agency. The issuance of stock also took Fannie Mae's finances off the government balance sheet, improving a budget picture beset by the Vietnam War and the Great Society social programs of the Johnson administration.

In 1970, the government created Freddie Mac to compete with Fannie Mae. It, too, was a GSE that had public shareholders.

In the years leading up to the housing crisis, rules restricting Fannie and Freddie's participation in the riskier subprime mortgage markets were eased, helping to fuel the increase in these kinds of mortgages. Government officials pressed both Fannie and Freddie to help less advantaged individuals to acquire homes. Some critics argue that this activity landed too many people in homes they ultimately couldn't afford, contributing to the housing crisis and the ensuing financial crisis.

With Fannie and Freddie aggressively acquiring risky mortgages, regular banks had to get more aggressive themselves. This led to a beggar-thy-neighbor environment that helped undercut mortgage discipline throughout the country. No money down? No problem. Don't want to pay your mortgage this month? No problem. Bad credit? No problem. A similar reduction in standards led individuals to pile up credit card debt and add to their traditional housing debt through additional mortgages and home-equity loans.

The comfort with all this housing-related debt stemmed from a single premise: housing prices would always go up, even if only a little. So what did lenders or borrowers have to worry about? A mortgage gone bad meant a bank could simply foreclose on the house and sell it back into the booming market. It might even make money on the deal.

The housing boom spread far beyond U.S. shores in a portent of the whirlwind to come. England, Ireland, Spain, Hungary, Turkey and other nations devoured borrowed money to drive housing booms. The easy-money policy of the Federal Reserve, coupled with excessive savings in the developing nations of Asia, led to an ocean of cash looking for opportunity. With interest rates low, real estate became the most likely home.

With the housing boom roaring, the tsunami of the financial crisis was starting to churn. The housing bonanza created oceans of debt that Wall Street could turn into investments of varying shapes and sizes. The Federal Reserve's low-interest-rate policy created oceans of easy money to pour into those investments. And the Wizards of Wall Street stood ready to turn even the most toxic combinations of debt, primarily of the subprime variety, into opportunities for hedge funds and other investors.

FAQ

What is a bubble?

This term is sometimes overused, with people applying it to any sharp rise in the prices of stocks or other assets. A bubble, by definition, is an overexuberant rise in asset prices that is ultimately unsustainable. A burst bubble causes enormous damage, and postbubble asset prices can struggle for a long time to reach previous highs. For instance, the stock prices of Internet companies remain a long way from the highs reached in 2000. Japanese stocks, nearly two decades after that country's bubble run, are still a fraction of their value at the height of the mania.

Do home values always rise?

No. In fact, they usually just stay even with inflation, historically rising about 3% a year. Housing prices have slumped in the past or, as in the case of the 1970s, struggled to keep pace with inflation. Home values are expected to remain weak for some time to come, which is common in the aftermath of bubblelike speculation.

Why did fear of risk diminish so completely?

It took some time. The erosion of fear occurred over more than 20 years. The quick rebound of the U.S. stock market after the 1987 crash, the rapid recovery of the Asian markets 10 years later and relatively mild recessions during

FAQ

this period slowly built confidence and reduced the fear of risk. This lack of fear helped companies and individuals persist in ill-considered behavior for an extended period of time, culminating in the financial crisis of 2007–2008.

Why do low interest rates matter?

The Federal Reserve controls short-term interest rates. High interest rates make it difficult to borrow money. When they are very low, as was the case in 2002 through 2004, borrowing becomes very easy which naturally reduces financial discipline. For instance, homeowners who found themselves struggling with debt or mortgage payments during the easy-money heyday could simply take out more debt from their home in order to make the payments. This layering of debt on top of debt, of course, made them more vulnerable to any downturn in home values.

TWO

FINANCIAL WIZARDRY

A COMBINATION OF MANY EVENTS led to the scenario in which Wall Street practically destroyed itself in an orgy of delusion and greed and transformed into something else entirely. Oh sure, Goldman Sachs and Morgan Stanley haven't disappeared. Merrill Lynch and Bear Stearns remain as part of much larger banks. But it's hard to imagine the swaggering, globe-trotting Wall Street Kings of the Universe returning anytime soon. It will take years just to assess and repair the damage, let alone restart—or, in this case, rebuild—the big Wall Street moneymaking machine that had so dominated global finance.

Wall Street's ultimate woe had its origins in an area it considered its biggest strength: its skill in devising financial products that hedged risks, drove fees and enriched the investment banks. Starting in the 1980s, the combination of the intelligence and technology on Wall Street helped to expand its complex array of risk-management products. These usually involved slicing, dicing and repackaging everything from pools of mortgages to the future earnings of David Bowie's songs. This financial expertise centered on anything that threw off a reasonably predictable cash flow. For instance, a pool of mortgages has a steady, expected string of payments stretching out over the life of the mortgages. This cash flow is predictable, to an extent, and the package of securities is priced based on the expected cash flow from the underlying instruments—in this case, the mortgages.

The creation of complex investment vehicles enriched Wall Street but also gave those on the Street a false sense of security. As the real estate boom unfolded, firms concocted ever more elaborate ways of extracting fees from the sector. On the surface, these instruments were aimed at mitigating risk. In reality, they injected enormous debt into the system, which would ultimately magnify the difficulties concomitant with a decline in real estate prices and overwhelm the system.

Wall Street firms, in the most basic terms, would package the debt attached to the cash flow of a pool of products, such as mortgages, credit card debt or auto loans, and "securitize" it, or sell it, to hedge funds, pension funds or other large investors. In theory, the holder of the securitized debt would get a return as long as the underlying debtors or, in some cases, a cash-generating project, such as a toll road, continued to generate money for the securitized debt holders.

Wall Street also dipped more heavily into elaborate investment products, such as the previously mentioned credit-default swaps and collateralized debt obligations, which essentially involved trading unregulated contracts outside regular exchanges. Such contracts were structured for a specific reason: for example, protecting against a corporation's defaulting on its debt, which was primarily covered by a credit-default swap (CDS). In other words, if you think Idaho Semiconductor is going to fail on its debt, and you hold some of that debt, you can buy a CDS as insurance against such a default. Should Idaho Semiconductor fail, the person who sold you the CDS would have to cover the default.

THE ALPHABET SOUP OF DERIVATIVES

Derivatives have been called financial "weapons of mass destruction" by the investor Warren Buffett and praised by others, such as former Federal Reserve chief Alan Greenspan, as important shock absorbers in the financial system. How can two such intelligent people have such divergent views about a single thing? Partly because derivatives are multifaceted and range from the very simple to the brain-poppingly complex. Some observers have described derivatives as being like a gun: perfectly fine in certain circumstances but deadly nonetheless.

At its most basic, a derivative is an investment that "derives" from an underlying security. For instance, oil is traded in "futures." An oil future gives a buyer the right to receive a delivery of oil at a specified future date. The future contract is a derivative of the underlying basket of oil. A stock option is another derivative.

As discussed previously, it gives buyers the opportunity to purchase a stock at a specific price at a specific point in time.

From those simple origins, financial wizards have concocted ever more complicated derivatives. And unlike futures and options, which trade on regulated exchanges, these derivatives exist in the mostly unregulated part of the market. In theory, these derivatives were meant to spread risk, making the financial system more resilient. In practice, many derivatives allowed for an increased amount of leverage, or borrowing, to pour into the financial system. The most common derivatives at the heart of the financial crisis are credit-default swaps (CDSs), collateralized debt obligations (CDOs) and collateralized mortgage obligations (CMOs). Others in the alphabet soup include mortgage-backed securities and other asset-backed securities.

A CDS provides the buyer with insurance against a debt default, if one should occur. A CDO pools debt of various stripes, in the current crisis usually mortgages, and sells them to investors in "tranches," which are essentially buckets of different types of debt of varying credit quality. Many of these CDOs were mysteriously given very high credit ratings even though their assets later proved to be anything but valuable. CMOs also seemed to get blessings far above their ultimate value. A lot of these ill-informed ratings stemmed from the single greatest false belief that fed the financial crisis: that real estate prices always go up, even if just a little. When real estate prices went down—a lot—most of these investments went badly awry. As a result, Buffett looks a lot smarter than Greenspan on this particular issue.

A CDS became a popular trading vehicle, primarily because corporate debt defaults were fairly rare in the years ahead of the financial crisis. In 2002, few people expected General Electric to default on its debt, but investors were happy to trade the likelihood of such a default (somewhere between tiny and small) among themselves, either to hedge a position in the company or to outright try to make money on expectations about GE's debt.

Investors hedge a position when they want to protect against its going south. For instance, if a hedge fund owns General Motors debt and is concerned that the company might fail, it would buy a CDS to provide a payout in case GM couldn't pay its debts. Once the credit crunch and global financial crisis took hold, making it a lot harder for even the most solid companies to pay their debts, these instruments, along with the alphabet soup of exotic financial products, stood at the center of the storm. And often, many of the CDSs and their even more complicated cousins had been purchased with borrowed money in the first place.

With the housing market roaring ahead in the early 2000s, Wall Street applied its skill with developing complex investment products to that market. First, homeowners were borrowing enormous amounts of money, a good deal of it in the risky subprime mortgage market. Second, long payback periods for mortgages (30 years in most cases) provided a steady stream of cash flow that made investors in securitized debt and related financial derivatives more excited.

Banks were happy to feed the Wall Street mortgage machine. They'd issue mortgages on houses and quickly sell them to a Wall Street firm, which would happily slice and dice the mortgages and repackage them into more complicated investment instruments. The banks, such as U.S. Bancorp and Wells Fargo, didn't have to worry about the long-term financial health of the mortgage borrowers, since those mortgages were now out of their hands and off their balance sheets. If Joe Borrower, on the other hand, got into financial trouble and couldn't make his mortgage payments, renegotiating a mortgage became a complex nightmare. Many borrowers found themselves in Joe's shoes. They had adjustable-rate mortgages that adjusted higher, they had taken out no-money-down mortgages or interest-only mortgages, where they didn't initially pay off any of their underlying mortgage debt. When housing prices started to fall, many of these mortgage holders found themselves with more mortgage debt than their house was now worth. In order to try and solve this conundrum, Joe and others tried to renegotiate their mortgage—but finding the new owner of the mortgage was well-nigh impossible. Indeed, by the time the mortgage emerged from firms like Merrill Lynch, Lehman Brothers and other Wall Street firms, it had multiple pieces with multiple owners in multiple countries, none of whom would be terribly interested in working out Joe's mortgage. This is one reason a mortgage rescue plan has proved so difficult to implement.

Wall Street hadn't noticed that mortgages made for good securitization only in 2002. Mortgage-backed securities were developed in the late 1970s and initially became popular in the 1980s and continued to grow through the 1990s. But this market really took off as the real estate craze grew from 2002 through 2006.

The boom in mortgage debt received a big boost from the

growth in subprime mortgages. These mortgages, usually issued to people with bad or no credit, once held little interest for investors. Securitizing them led to high yields (the interest rate paid on an investment). But though the yields were high, so too was the risk that the subprime borrowers would default on their mortgages. Wall Street didn't precisely know what to do with all this lousy mortgage debt until eventually . . . it did.

As the housing market took off in 2002, investors became increasingly hungry for yield. Yield is the interest-rate return on an investment. A common reference point is the yield, or interest paid, on a 10-year Treasury bond, which was just under 3% at the end of 2008. The Federal Reserve had lowered short-term interest rates to 1% in 2003 to fight an economic slow-down. That made it very challenging to find high-interest-rate investments that weren't extraordinarily risky (which subprime mortgages certainly were). With interest rates so low, safe investments such as Treasurys yielded puny interest rates. These low rates, however, helped propel the housing market to even stronger growth. The reason: low interest rates made the cost of financing a home purchase much easier. It was, in a sense, easy money. This easy money emboldened individuals to buy bigger homes, since the monthly payments seemed relatively reasonable due to the low-interest-rate environment.

The boom in mortgages, especially subprime mortgages, presented Wall Street with a challenge: how to effectively monetize this risky, high-yielding debt in a way that would attract the most buyers. The solution to this dilemma was audacious: financial wizards working at all the big investment banks—

Cheap Money Extends Credit and Risk Expands to Match

Lower rates for U.S. borrowers...

U.S. federal-funds interest-rate target, the short-term lending benchmark

And foreign appetite for U.S. debt...

Net foreign purchases of U.S. debt securities, including Treasurys, agencies and corporate bonds

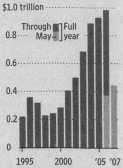

Sources: Federal Reserve; U.S. Treasury Department; Inside Mortgage Finance; UBS; Dealogic

Encouraged lending to less-qualified home buyers...

Subprime-mortgage originations

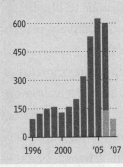

On increasingly risky terms...

The ratio of loans to property value rose and more loans were made to borrowers with less-than-full documentation; subprime loans only

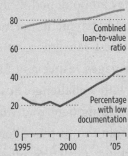

Fueling new kinds of investment

Collateralized debt obligations issued

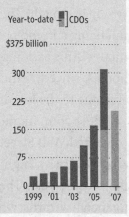

Goldman Sachs, Morgan Stanley, Bear Stearns, Merrill Lynch, Lehman Brothers—concocted instruments that magically transformed subprime mortgage debt into something far more attractive.

In simple terms, they took all kinds of mortgage debt—subprime, top-rated, and so on—and threw them into a huge pot. They then swirled the debt around, stirred it and repackaged it into various bundles that bore all kinds of fancy names: collateralized mortgage obligations, collateralized debt obligations and so on.

Even though a huge amount of foul-smelling debt had been tossed into the barrel, when it came out in these repackaged bundles, the ratings agencies declared the debt top-rated. Since, of course, there was no shortage of fishy debt at the bottom of the repackaged CMO or CDO, the interest rate, or yield, on the repackaged debt was nice and high. It was amazingly simple and, by some measures, deceitful. The ratings agencies played along with this game, happily rating everything that came out of the Wall Street investment bank mulchers as good investments, as though the reality itself could be morphed by the power of spreadsheets and computers.

Of course, the ratings agencies suffered from the same complacent conceit that affected the entire industry. "Real estate prices always go up, even if just a little." If that's the assumption, it becomes pretty natural to go easy on rating all real estate–related debt. Michael Lewis, writing in Portfolio magazine, recounts how one rating agency didn't allow for real estate price declines in its modeling.

THE RATINGS AGENCIES

Scratch a recent financial crisis, and inevitably you will find the ratings agencies. Such agencies are charged with assessing the risk of various debt issues and then giving them a rating. So, when General Motors sells corporate bonds, the ratings agencies examine General Motors' books and the nature of the bond issue and then slap a rating on the offering.

This sounds simple enough. So it is confounding that the ratings agencies so frequently miss potential trouble. The list of missed calls includes spectacular corporate collapses such as Enron and WorldCom.

The dominant players in the market are Standard & Poor's and Moody's Investors Service. Fitch Ratings is also in the market, but its market share is much smaller. These firms are widely considered sober-minded, green-eyeshade types. In a quirk of the system, the ratings agencies are paid by the companies that are being rated or need a rating, in the case of a Wall Street firm issuing a new form of debt, creating a potential conflict of interest.

Upon review, it's clear that the ratings agencies gave top ratings to debt comprised of mostly terrible assets. It's still a mystery as to how that took place. Ratings agencies, of course, aren't expected to be perfect. But if they had not given their seal of approval, a lot of the dreckish derivatives that contributed to the financial crisis wouldn't have come to market.

The ease with which all of the mortgages, especially lousy ones, were repackaged and sent out into the system helped drive rapid growth. The Fed's easy-money policy didn't hurt, either. That policy not only made it a cinch for individuals to buy homes at low interest rates; it also enabled investors to use more and more borrowed money to buy all the repackaged mortgages that flowed from the housing boom.

As with all manias, things can carry on for quite some time before everyone discovers that the emperor's wearing no clothes. In retrospect, the Internet and tech stock bubble really got out of hand in 1998 when the Nasdaq Composite Index stood at about 2000, a level it has struggled to reach since crashing in 2001. Looking at a long time chart, a rational observer can declare: Right there was where it went nuts.

But in 1998 that period of "nuts" for the Nasdaq Composite still has more than two years to run. That's an eternity on Wall Street. Fund managers who are essentially "wrong" for two years get fired—eventually. Wall Street CEOs who are "wrong"

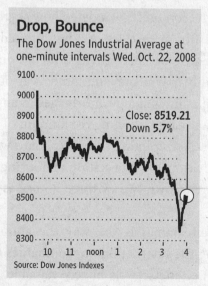

Drop, Bounce
The Dow Jones Industrial Average at one-minute intervals Wed. Oct. 22, 2008

Close: 8519.21
Down 5.7%

Source: Dow Jones Indexes

for two years find themselves alone on the golf course—but not right away. Knowing that something has gone crazy and knowing when everyone will notice are two different things.

So, in our recent experience, the real estate party ran along fairly nicely for some time. From 2000 through 2004, real estate was on everyone's minds. High-risk mortgage holders kept making their payments, and the multifarious repackaged debt instruments seemed to be working just fine. The financial firms felt increasingly confident in the complex debt-related contraptions they had built and took on more and more risk. Banks, eager to earn more money and keep the mortgage boom rolling, trimmed back lending standards to draw more business. The real estate gravy train became a juggernaut.

Critics argued in 2003 that lending standards had become too lax. By 2004, economists wondered how skyrocketing home values could justify themselves. Analysts fretted about the exotica of mortgage loans that provided for no down payments, optional monthly payments and other various newfangled methods aimed at moving new mortgages in any possible way. Planners also started questioning the amount of housing pouring onto the market. It didn't seem to square with population growth or any reasonable expectation of housing demand, even if everyone were to own two or three homes as well as two or three cars.

A sign of all manias is the way the abnormal becomes normal. During the Internet boom, companies that had yet to make a profit became seen as hugely valuable, far more than companies making money. That, of course, made very little sense. In the case of real estate, nonsense abounded. Mortgage lenders became so aggressive that unemployed people with no credit found ways to finance home purchases. Those assessing home values for home-equity loans or home-equity lines of credit simply increased the appraised value of a home without much rigor, blindly counting on the assumption of always-rising real estate prices. No restrictions, optional payments, generous appraisals: anything to keep the mortgage boom going.

It's important to note that the real estate craziness spread to other areas of the debt market. Companies found themselves able to borrow with minimal collateral. Acquisitions financed by banks historically had many performance covenants to protect the lenders. As debt discipline diminished, these covenants disappeared. In a world of easy money—easy for real estate, easy for companies, easy for deals—lenders found themselves fighting desperately to win business. All this led to two things: a collapse in standards and an explosion in lending.

The collapse in standards played out prominently in the corporate acquisition market. Private-equity firms borrowed large sums to acquire companies. Previously, such borrowing had required the borrower to meet certain performance measures in order to protect the lender. But money became so easy that these standards were reduced and, in many cases, simply eliminated. These deals—called "covenant-light" financings—included several large buyouts, such as Kohlberg Kravis Roberts' (KKR) $26 billion purchase of First Data in April 2007.

On Wall Street, the slowly rising litany of concerns about

PRIVATE-EQUITY FUNDS

The private-equity fund business must have some excellent marketers. The term "private equity" sounds benign and sober, when, in fact, the private-equity world is one of high intensity, brutal cost cutting and ferocious capitalism. In an earlier age, people referred to such funds as "leveraged buyout funds," or LBOs. But LBOs got a bad name when many of their companies went bust in the late 1980s and early 1990s.

Big players in this space, such as KKR, the Blackstone Group, Texas Pacific Group (TPG), the Carlyle Group and Goldman Sachs. One of the most famous private-equity deals remains KKR's $25 billion acquisition of RJR Nabisco in 1985, the subject of the book *Barbarians at the Gate* by Bryan Burrough and John Helyar, which highlighted the excesses of the 1980s market boom. KKR, partnering with TPG, surpassed this deal when it acquired the utility company TXU Corp. for $45 billion in 2007.

Private-equity funds acquire companies or divisions of companies with an eye toward fixing these companies and then later reselling them, either to another company or to the public via an initial public offering. The word "private" in their name stems from their frequent habit of taking over publicly traded companies and making them private.

When making such an acquisition, a private-equity fund borrows lots of money to fund the purchase and then uses the cash flow of the acquired company to fund the debt. Since such companies quickly become highly leveraged, that is, they have a lot of debt, their bonds are generally rated as "junk," as opposed to the investment-grade bonds that blue-chip companies such as IBM would issue.

With interest rates very low during the post-Internet bubble era and borrowing exceedingly easy, private-equity funds boomed. They raised hundreds of billions of dollars and acquired a large number of companies. Not satisfied to play the typical quieter game of buying and turning around smallish companies or divisions of companies, these funds bought huge, big-name companies such as Burger King, the health-care giant HCA and the casino operator Harrah's Entertainment. Deal volume soared to nearly $800 billion in 2006 from a measly $34 billion ten years earlier.

That deal boom has, of course, faded quickly amid the financial turmoil. And now many of these highly leveraged companies face challenging debt payments ahead. Private-equity players even used their borrowing strategies to invest in other areas, such as English soccer teams. Those indebted teams now also face an uncertain future.

Private-equity firms boasted that by taking companies private they could focus on improving operating performance without the burden of reporting results, as a publicly traded company must do. This claim seemed ironic, to be charitable, when Blackstone, one of the biggest private-equity players, took itself public in 2007 earning its chief Stephen Schwarzman $800 million. The Blackstone IPO, in retrospect, quite possibly signaled the end of the private-equity boom and foreshadowed much tougher times ahead.

the debt market, especially in real estate, hardly dented confidence. And it led to willful acts of greed that in retrospect look downright foolish. Wall Street firms, which had boasted about their ability to spread risk around in the wake of the telecom debt implosions of the early 2000s, started taking on more risk rather than spreading it. The reason? The products they had created to spread risk were performing so well that it was more profitable to keep the products than to sell them off to other investors.

Throughout the 2000s, Wall Street firms had bragged about distributing risk rapidly around the world to small banks, college endowments, unions and other investors. This risk spreading enabled the industry to weather cataclysmic moments, such as the aforementioned telecom debt collapse of 2000–2001. In theory, by spreading the risk far and wide, when things went bad everyone would lose just a little rather than a single entity losing everything.

But the financial experts had done such a good job of masking the dangers of real estate debt, making it a valuable investment in and of itself because of its unusually high yields, that it became very tempting to hold some of the investments in-house, rather than sell them. Why not get a little greedy? Of course, this greed peaked around 2006 and 2007, just as things started to go awry in the real estate markets. At this time many Wall Street firms became risk gatherers as opposed to risk spreaders. And, of course, they had acquired these debt-laden assets with borrowing of their own. Clever, clever. Borrowing upon borrowing to buy assets based on borrowing. This kind of leveraging is a great strategy when you're right, because the borrowing amplifies your gains. When you are wrong, as we have learned, Katy, bar the door.

Questions about the sustainability of the housing boom rose sharply in 2005 and into 2006. Statements that the boom had become a bubble proliferated. But the reality of a bubble ripe for a nasty burst dissuaded few from participating heavily in the craziness. Among others, Merrill Lynch, Citigroup and Lehman Brothers continued to add mortgage-related debts aggressively to their balance sheets in 2007, even as it became clear even to casual observers that the real estate market had taken a dark turn. Whether hope trumped logic or simple inertia took hold, the inability to change direction fated many firms to disaster.

The year 2006 ended in a simple enough way. Real estate prices had started to slip in some parts of the country, but the slippage remained "contained" to bad debt—the subprime stuff buried in a lot of those complicated investment instruments. The stock market had a surprisingly healthy tone—it would rise through much of 2007, ticking above 14,000 in the summer. Merger and acquisition activity continued its strong pace, and takeover firms were busy raising tens of billions of dollars of new funds to acquire companies. Some takeover firms—the private-equity funds—were even taking themselves public. Hedge funds kept raking in cash, and their chiefs kept earning unheard-of sums. John Paulson, who runs Harbinger Capital, reportedly made $3 billion in 2007 and Steve Cohen, head of SAC Capital, raked in more than $1 billion.

As 2007 closed with booming bonuses and talk of great things to come, few observers would have predicted that Wall Street stood on the precipice of disaster and that soon the entire financial system would teeter, for some days, precariously on the verge of collapse.

Some, of course, could see parts of what was to come, even if the whole picture was not yet clear. Robert Shiller, the Yale economist who had correctly forecast the demise of the Internet Bubble, now talked darkly about the real estate market entering a similar phase. Ian Shepherdson, an economist at High Frequency Economics, a consultancy, saw real estate problems leading into a deep recession. Nouriel Roubini, an economist at New York University, foresaw problems in both the economy and the securitization markets. Despite their prescience, they were like the blind men of the fable, each holding on to a different part of the elephant. Not one of them could see the entire beast about to stampede in its full and terrible glory.

One reason it was difficult to see the full extent of the looming problems is that the unchecked use of leverage seeped into the system in many ways, facilitated by the financial engineers on Wall Street. This leverage, basically the borrowing of money to amplify an investment bet, became excessive and would eventually nearly overwhelm the system itself. The sources of the leverage were manifold. For starters, developing nations, especially in Asia, had an abundance of savings. Rather than spend or invest that money at home, much of those savings made their way to the U.S., where they became part of the debt-building machine. The easiest way this occurred was with the purchase of U.S. Treasury debt or so-called agency debt, such as that issued by Fannie Mae and Freddie Mac, the mortgage giants with a government-implied backing.

Under some theories, the heavy investment by developing nations in Treasurys and agency debt pushed interest rates on that debt lower, thereby making other debt interest payments lower. This prompted investors to search eagerly for higher

ROBERT SHILLER

Robert Shiller is a Yale economist who has distinguished himself twice for forecasting investment troubles ahead. During the tail end of the 1990s stock market boom, he persuasively argued that the stock market had become a bubble and would have a bad ending. He buttressed this call by publishing a book, *Irrational Exuberance,* in 2000, just before the bottom fell out of the market.

Subsequently, Shiller has focused on the real estate market. Doing substantial research, he showed that home values over the past 100 years have usually risen about in line with inflation, making the double-digit gains of the early part of the decade seem nonsensical. He argued in 2005 that the current home price increases were not sustainable. He was right about that, too.

He has worked on solving an interesting riddle: how to "hedge" real estate. Unlike many other investments, it is nearly impossible to insure, or hedge, the value of your house. His research helped lead to the creation of home-value indexes for major cities that trade on the Chicago Mercantile Exchange. In theory, one could use these indexes to hedge one's home, but they are still too expensive and complex for most individual homeowners to utilize.

yield or interest payments on investments. This mind-set helped investors overlook the chicanery taking place on Wall Street as firms developed surprisingly high-yielding products with supposedly highly rated underlying debt.

The financial engineers also found additional ways to add leverage to the system. The alphabet soup of securitized instruments often depended on leveraged assets. The hedge funds that bought the leveraged assets borrowed money to do so. Sometimes investors in hedge funds were investing with borrowed cash. And the investment banks working alongside the hedge funds on various deals borrowed $25, $30, sometimes $35 for each dollar they actually held. This use of borrowed funds meant that investment banks and hedge funds could buy 20 or 30 times as much product as they could if they had used their cash only to make investments. For instance, if a hedge fund thought General Electric would gain 5% in value, it could borrow 30 dollars for each dollar of cash it wanted to invest and thereby multiply the potential return by 30. Of course, that multiplier effect also works in reverse.

Debt upon debt upon debt, much of it tied to real estate— which itself had become an enormous source of borrowing and leverage—piled up. Like a Rube Goldberg machine, each action and reaction seemed to require just a bit more debt and a bit more borrowing to work. At the origin of the crisis, real estate played the cat on the treadmill. As long as it kept running, everything would be okay.

But by early 2007, the cat had gotten tired.

FAQ

Have financial derivatives created problems in the past?

Yes. In the 1990s, a surprising shift in interest rates caught many investors in financial derivatives off balance. Most notably, the Orange County government found itself filing for bankruptcy after a derivatives bet went awry. Some companies, such as Gibson Greetings, the card maker acquired by American Greetings in 2000, also got caught up in the mess. Gibson made several speculative derivative investments and reported losses of more than $25 million from the investments in 1994. They invested in derivative products that did not perform as promised, losing millions in the process.

Why are financial derivatives so popular?

They can do many things, including hedging against a future loss or giving investors a chance to invest in something in the future. As with any financial instrument, derivatives can work for good or ill; the instrument itself is morally neutral. A good example of a derivative that makes sense is corn futures. A farmer can sell his crop, or a portion of his crop, in advance of the harvest, thereby locking in gains before going to market with the corn. Also, Southwest Airlines used oil price futures to help it lock in better prices for jet fuel than its competitors' when oil prices soared in 2006 and 2007.

FAQ

When did financial wizardry become popular?

In the 1970s, academicians came up with a formula to efficiently price stock options. This formula, called Black/Scholes after the academics who created it, powered the growth of stock options markets. In addition, options upon options and other various derivatives upon derivatives soon followed suit. The increase in computing power during this period had an immense impact on the growth of financial derivatives.

THREE

CANARIES

O NE OF THE CURIOUS aspects of the current financial crisis is its slow-motion buildup and dramatic apogee over the course of a bit more than a year. What happened was not dissimilar to what can happen in a coal mine, where toxic gas can seep unseen into the work spaces, eventually killing the miners. That's why miners learned to keep canaries deep underground, because the birds would die first from the unseen, unsmelled gas, giving the miners a chance to escape.

On Wall Street, canaries abounded as far back as late 2006 as the subprime problems began to surface and home values began to decline. But manias make it difficult to see or hear clearly, as was the case during the Internet stock bubble. And because of the size of the problems facing banks and other financial firms, finding solutions to the crisis proved very difficult, even though there was time to try to find it. Lehman Brothers knew it faced significant solvency issues for more than a year, but it couldn't raise enough capital to offset its enormous amount of bad debts. Similarly, those at Bear Stearns and mortgage lenders such as Washington Mutual, Countrywide Financial and IndyMac Federal Bank knew they faced problems. But most observers think that the crisis unfolded at a comparatively leisurely pace, giving those involved ample time to find solutions before the tsunami hit in September 2008.

If there is a string to pull that can take us back to the origins of the crisis, it is the start of the subprime lending market troubles. Toward the end of 2006 and into early 2007, individual homeowners began to fail on their subprime loans. Little wonder: many of these people had qualified for a loan simply by having a pulse and a pen. But since everyone was buying the premise that "real estate prices always go up," if the borrower failed, the bank would just take over the house and resell it at a profit. Given that mind-set, everyone qualified for a subprime mortgage. And everyone, it seems, applied.

As the subprime borrowers defaulted, those defaults led to foreclosures, an unfamiliar sight during the housing boom. The first foreclosures also pierced the mythology around rising home prices. If some homeowners couldn't hang on to their homes, either by keeping up with their mortgages or, as had been the case at the height of the mania, borrowing still more on their homes to keep up the payments, then maybe homes weren't the magical perfect investment. After an early trickle, foreclosures soared to record levels during the real estate crisis.

By early 2008, foreclosures outnumbered actual home sales in once booming Orange County, California.

The subprime defaults rippled through the array of mortgage-related debt securities Wall Street had concocted during the housing boom. These securities were held by pension funds, hedge funds and, as became painfully clear in the ensuing months, banks and investment banks as well. Many of these debts were far more toxic than advertised, almost entirely dependent on rising real estate prices. As the subprime failures mounted, the illogic and unsustainability of the arrangement became clearer. Subprime defaults rippled through the array of mortgage-related debt securities Wall Street had concocted during the housing boom.

Remarkably, what was soon called the "subprime meltdown" caused little more than the usual concern on Wall Street or among investors. The Dow Jones Industrial Average plumped to a record close above 14,000 in October 2007, even as the subprime problems metastasized. Most observers felt that since housing prices would continue to rise, or at least not go down very much before recovering, the subprime crisis would solve itself without causing widespread damage to the financial system or the markets.

But then home values began to drop more steadily—not everywhere and not all at once, but enough to augment the chain of events the subprime crisis had started. Indeed, the decline in home values began to threaten so-called non-subprime mortgages. A bit too much supply in Las Vegas helped press prices lower. Too few interested buyers in coastal Florida did the same. Falling home values and a rising number of subprime and other mortgage failures made lenders start to get a bit tougher about their lending standards. A frisson of fear flickered in the once impervious housing market. Real estate prices are highly localized, so drawing any national conclusions is challenging, but it's clear that the market had topped and was starting to turn over in many places.

Home prices continued to drop as 2007 unfolded and rumors of difficulties in the finance sector grew. This was surprising at first, since real estate prices hadn't fallen that much, just a couple of percentage points year over year. By the end of 2007, things had grown much worse, with overall home prices declining by nearly 9% year over year, the worst performance in more than 20 years. In early 2007, however, few people fully understood two things: the extent of borrowing associated with real estate and the amount of complex, questionably rated debt assets tied to that debt that depended essentially on rising real estate prices.

During the summer of 2007, more canaries died. Hedge funds run by the large French bank BNP Paribas and Wall Street investment bank Bear Stearns ran into trouble and ultimately failed. The problem at both: bad real estate-related debt holdings, an ominous indicator of what was ahead, even though investors largely ignored the fund failures, propelling stocks still higher. The swift demise of the funds came ahead of what economists expected would be a rapidly worsening residential real estate market, especially in places such as Florida, California and Nevada.

The slowly shifting environment led to modest changes in lending practices. Banks got just a mite tougher with one another, especially with banks heavily dependent on mortgage debt. Lending practices went from insanely generous to merely generous. But this shift alone created problems in unexpected places. It seemed that some banks had become addicted to short-term financing. In other words, to keep the wheels rolling, they needed to keep going to the debt markets. It was the classic Wimpy philosophy of Popeye fame: I will gladly pay you Tuesday for a hamburger today.

Amazingly, the first big casualty of the U.S. housing and associated financial engineering debacle fell in a foreign land. As home prices fell in Los Angeles and Miami, a plucky bank in the north of England began to get nervous. Northern Rock, a surprising success story during the U.K. property boom of the late 1990s and 2000s had done well enough to become a jersey sponsor of the top-level Newcastle United Football Club. Each week, tens of millions of people around the world watched Newcastle United, making Northern Rock a bit of a brand name even beyond the U.K.

Northern Rock had dined lavishly at the real estate table, investing heavily in real estate debt and lending aggressively to developers. Like the U.S. and many other developed countries, the U.K. was in the midst of a real estate boom, and Northern Rock was heavily involved in the boom.

As the subprime crisis in the U.S. accelerated, fears of real estate–related problems spread quickly around the globe. By the summer of 2007, lending standards everywhere had started to tighten—both for individuals and for banks, most of which rely on their ability to borrow from one another. Dependent on short-term debt to fund its operations, Northern Rock found itself particularly vulnerable to a sudden credit squeeze.

Unlike the U.S., the U.K. had no bank deposit insurance at the time (it later instituted a temporary version of deposit insurance during the height of the crisis). Since the Great Depression, the U.S. has insured bank deposits in the case of bank failure, meaning that those with accounts in a failed bank will still get their money despite the bank's failure. Whispers of Northern Rock's difficulties in meeting near-term debt payments led nervous individuals to worry about the money they had deposited in Northern Rock. By September 2007, an old-fashioned bank run had started, and lines of depositors encircled Northern Rock branches, trying to get their money. In a sign of the confusing policy responses that would mark the initial phases of the financial crisis, the British government initially declined to intervene to save Northern Rock or to protect its depositors by either investing in Northern Rock or guaranteeing deposits at the bank. Eventually the bank was nationalized and the deposits were guaranteed, but that resolution took some months.

The surprising bank run at Northern Rock led many in the U.S. to start worrying about whether such an event could happen here. Investors started more closely scouring the balance sheets of real estate–centric companies such as Fannie Mae, Freddie Mac, Countrywide, IndyMac, Washington Mutual and Wachovia. In addition, big players in the securitization of mortgage-related debt, such as Bear Stearns, Lehman Brothers, Citigroup and Merrill Lynch, came in for more scrutiny.

BANK RUNS

Until recently, bank runs for most folks existed only in the movies, primarily the Christmas film *It's a Wonderful Life.* The main character, George Bailey's, humble building and loan suffers a massive bank run, and despite his efforts to explain how a bank works, the good people of Bedford Falls simply want all their money back. He survives the run thanks to help from the community he has so faithfully served. Great story. Too bad it doesn't always work that way.

Banks typically keep just a scant amount of their deposits, usually around 10%, in accessible accounts. The rest of the deposits are loaned out to home buyers, college students, auto buyers, businesses and others who require debt. This is how the bank makes money with your money. The compact between banker and depositor is that the bank will manage your money intelligently and always be there when you want to take your money out.

But since banks don't always have easy access to all your money, they are vulnerable to a run. In this scenario, nervous depositors converge all at once on a bank and ask for their money back. In a "minirun," a bank can access money from the Federal Reserve System to provide money for withdrawals. Since a run is primarily the product of lost confidence, a bank's ability to pay out on a minirun usually calms the depositors and the panic subsides.

In more serious situations, the FDIC, which insures deposit accounts, can step in and take over the bank and transfer deposits to a healthier institution. Because of the insurance system in place, bank runs have become exceedingly rare, even if bank failures have not. In Great Britain, the run on Northern Rock in 2007 led the government to nationalize the bank. Northern Rock, heavily exposed to bad real estate debt, was one of the first casualties of the financial crisis.

Some have described the collapse of Bear Stearns and Lehman Brothers as akin to a run on a bank. Fearing the failure of the firms, investors demanded their cash back and others in the financial markets declined to trade or deal with the firms. This herd movement is, in essence, the same mentality that takes place during a typical run on a bank.

Some of the worst bank runs in the U.S. came during the early part of the Great Depression. Several economists blame these runs and subsequent massive bank failures as playing a large role in the Great Depression.

The run on Northern Rock focused minds and led to a single question: Was this a simple subprime crisis or something worse? After all, bank runs, like the one suffered by Northern Rock, are exceedingly rare. Analysts at Wall Street firms and within the Federal Reserve tried to quantify the amount of bad mortgage-related debt ticking away on balance sheets like time bombs. At first it was some hundreds of billions of dollars. As home prices kept dropping, the figures kept rising. The total figure of bad debt remains elusive, but estimates ultimately ranged over $1 trillion.

The mortgage giant Countrywide, saddled with failing mortgage debts and seeing few avenues of exit, became the next to fall, selling itself to Bank of America at a rock-bottom price in early 2008. Bank of America, as it acquired more and more troubled firms and assets during the course of the crisis, including Merrill Lynch, was often referred to as *the* Bank of America, as though none other existed.

In the wake of the Northern Rock run, policy makers began to take more concerted action to add liquidity to the financial system. The Federal Reserve and European Central Bank injected hundreds of billions of dollars and euros into the system in the last two quarters of 2007. The Fed also started to contemplate more creative uses of its assets to help troubled firms recover. Eventually, the Fed would take on billions of dollars' worth of toxic debt as collateral and even move to back a commercial paper funding facility that topped $1.3 trillion in estimated value.

THE FEDERAL RESERVE SYSTEM

The Federal Reserve System, the U.S. central bank, has become an overwhelmingly influential player in the financial crisis. It has created a number of lending programs to try to stave off disaster, and it has frequently intervened to force mergers and buttress surviving financial institutions. Its creativity in trying to solve the crisis has surprised some people. The success of its efforts remains an open question. Its balance sheet is now littered with questionable assets related to its manifold rescue efforts.

The outsized role of the Fed in the past two years stands in sharp contrast to most of its history. A central banker is supposed to be dull, sober and quietly reassuring. Until, that is, events warrant otherwise.

Founded in 1913, the Fed manages the nation's banking system. Its policy-making body also sets short-term interest rates, a powerful lever on the economy since those interest rates affect the manner in which banks lend. In theory, the Fed raises interest rates when the economy is booming and lowers them when the economy is wilting.

The Fed system is set up in a manner that made sense in 1913, when much of the nation's population lived east of the Mississippi. Today it looks a bit quaint. Of the 12 regional Fed banks, two are in Missouri, in Kansas City and St. Louis. West of Dallas, there's only one Fed bank, in San Francisco.

The New York Fed, given its direct role in the nation's financial capital, is the most powerful and important of the regional banks. Its president, Timothy Geithner, has worked very closely with Fed Chairman Ben Bernanke and Treasury Secretary Henry Paulson to combat the financial crisis. Following the recent election, President-elect Obama announced he would name Mr. Geithner as his Treasury secretary, succeeding Mr. Paulson.

The Federal Reserve is independent in its operations, meaning that politicians have no direct influence on its actions. Still, Congress has mandated through law that the Fed work to keep inflation low and employment high. The Fed chief is often called before Congress to report on how he's doing in meeting these mandates.

The Fed has had only three chairmen in the past 30 years: Paul Volcker, Alan Greenspan and Ben Bernanke.

Finally the boards of Wall Street firms started to take action. In November 2007, Merrill Lynch tossed Stan O'Neal, its CEO, and brought in John Thain, formerly head of the New York Stock Exchange. Merrill's write-downs (the process of acknowledging investments that had gone bad) ballooned just weeks after Mr. Thain's arrival, and he embarked on a capital-raising program. Write-downs and the raising of capital became the order of the day on Wall Street. Since so many investments had gone bad and many of those investments had been made with borrowed money, capital was needed to maintain solvency. Like bailing water from a sinking boat, executives were in a desperate race to solve the toxic real estate problem before it was too late.

During this bailing process, which continued deep into 2008, banks grabbed for capital far and wide. In December 2007, Merrill Lynch raised $6 billion from investors, among them Temasek Holdings, the investment arm of the Singaporean government. Citigroup raised $7.5 billion from Abu Dhabi in late 2007. Goldman Sachs raised $5 billion from Warren Buffett and others in September 2008. General Electric tapped Warren Buffett for $3 billion at the same time. But for many of the firms, the water of bad debt was rising more quickly than the bailers could bail.

CAPITAL-RAISING PROGRAMS AND WRITE-DOWNS

As debt-riddled investments went awry at investment and commercial banks during the financial crisis, a drive to raise additional capital became prevalent. Since banks didn't have enough capital on their balance sheets to cover their liabilities, not only did they seek more capital, they also aggressively "wrote down" their bad debt, essentially saying that the debts couldn't be fully recouped.

The bid for more capital led banks to seek cash from so-called sovereign wealth funds, or funds controlled by governments. Many of these funds are clustered around the oil-rich Persian Gulf, meaning that Kuwait, Abu Dhabi and Dubai became big investors in ailing U.S. commercial and investment banks. Other funds in Asia, such as Singapore's Temasek Holdings, banks in Japan and investment vehicles in China also plowed capital into the ailing U.S. financial companies.

For some companies, such as Morgan Stanley, enough money was raised to stave off collapse. In the case of Merrill Lynch, however, not enough capital was available to forestall it being sold to Bank of America.

At Bear Stearns, the race seemed lost from the start. After one of its hedge funds collapsed in the summer of 2007, critics argued that the firm hadn't done enough to reduce its exposure to toxic real estate debt and that its CEO, James Cayne, had become too detached from the business. *The Wall Street Journal* wrote about his isolation and frequent bridge tournaments to highlight a distracted CEO in time of crisis. The company's share price, at $171 in early 2007, fell sharply in the early part of 2008, and questions arose about the firm's ability to stay in business.

The issue of confidence plays a central role on Wall Street. Trades rely on verbal commitments, and investors must have faith that the other side of the deal, the "counterparty," will be good on the transaction. In simple terms, it's a great deal like buying a car. If you have concerns about the viability of an automaker, you are likely to hesitate. That's because the automaker provides warranties, parts and other important things that ensure the health of the car over the long term.

In Wall Street parlance, a firm is quite literally "good" until it's not. That's because once it's not, the game is over. The change can occur with radical speed. As in a bank run, confidence means everything: no confidence, no future. Bear Stearns faced such a situation in March 2008.

The venerable firm, once famous for its risk-management acumen, found itself begging the Street to believe it was healthy and posed no counterparty risk. As little as two days before its failure, Bear Stearns publicly declared that it was in excellent shape. Nobody believed it. Hedge funds and other Wall Street banks began to refuse to do business with Bear, and, rapidly withdrawing assets, the Street forced Bear to its knees. With the support of the government, J.P. Morgan Chase, which, like Bank of America, had become an acquirer of last resort during the crisis, bought Bear Stearns for $2 a share, or $236 million. Eventually that price rose to $10 a share after a number of Bear shareholders squawked.

Bear became the first Wall Street casualty, and most observers expressed surprise. Something had clearly gone wrong in its risk-management efforts since the firm had found itself lugging more bad debts than it could withstand. Instead of saving paper

BEAR STEARNS

Bear Stearns emerged in the 1990s and 2000s as an unlikely survivor in the tenacious world of global investment banking. From modest beginnings in the 1920s, Bear spurned combinations and built its business steadily with a heavy dollop of idiosyncrasy. Tellingly, Bear was one of the few surviving Wall Street firms that didn't lay anyone off after the Crash of 1929 and the ensuing depression. Indeed, Bear continued to expand its business modestly amid the wreckage.

This history bespoke Bear's strong record of risk management. Many on Wall Street considered Bear the shrewdest of dealers, able to snuff out problems where others saw no risk. The company cemented this reputation during the Long-Term Capital Management collapse, fighting tooth and nail to cover its own risk in LTCM before helping anyone else out. Indeed, in the end Bear did very little to help the overall LTCM rescue effort.

Bear continued to grow through the 1990s and into the 2000s, based on three main factors. First, it had a strong fixed-income business and was a dominant trader in that market, helping drive strong trading revenue both domestically and overseas. The firm also handled a great deal of hedge fund business through its "prime brokerage" arm. The prime brokers help hedge funds transact trades and manage accounts. Bear, along with Goldman Sachs, dominated this marketplace. Last, Bear, like other firms, increasingly traded often for its own account. Shortly before its demise, Bear carried leverage ratios of more than 30 to 1, meaning that for every dollar invested in the markets, it was borrowing 30 more to multiply those investments.

This massive amount of leverage seemed to contradict the famously thrifty image Bear had built over the decades. Alan "Ace"

Greenberg, the longtime chairman, answered his own phone and sent out memos about saving paper clips. Unlike many other Wall Street firms, Bear had an ethos that any hardworking, clever lad or lady could make it big there.

J.P. Morgan Chase, the heir to the great J.P. Morgan dynasty, acquired Bear Stearns in the spring of 2008 for $10 a share and guarantees from the Federal Reserve concerning Bear's large debt. The original deal offered Bear shareholders just $2 a share.

Like so many firms, Bear had bet big and badly on mortgage debt securities, especially those in the subprime space. As those securities continued to decline, Bear Stearns essentially went bankrupt—an ignominious end for a firm that had battled the tides to stay fiercely independent for more than eight decades.

clips, as its former, longtime CEO Alan "Ace" Greenberg had bragged it did, Bear had gobbled too heartily at the mortgage trough.

The slow and steady mortgage crisis seemed to take a breather as it digested Bear Stearns. Some believed that Bear marked the "sacrifice" to the market gods required to emerge from a crisis. But such mythology didn't gain much traction.

Questions were raised about the large and active role of the government in saving Bear—the Fed guaranteed $29 billion of Bear debt to help seal the deal. Did this mean that the Fed and others saw deeper, more systemic problems ahead? In other words, did the rescue occur because the risk of failure seemed too scary?

Looking back, the debates about the government's role in

the J.P. Morgan takeover seem quaint, given the enormity of what followed. Still, the rescue bore the ingredients of many future moves. The Fed intervenes to offer some guarantees. The Fed pushes the wilting seller into the arms of a bigger, healthier buyer, rather than let it fail outright. Last, the Fed uses its balance sheet aggressively to help deal with some of the toxic mortgage-related debts at the heart of the financial crisis.

After the Bear Stearns rescue, the credit markets continued to tighten. Lenders grew more and more leery of lending to one another, and the issuance of everything from car loans to mortgages slowed measurably. This credit crunch became the focus of policy makers and laid the groundwork for the autumn of failure on the horizon.

Though the stock markets, sometimes called the equity markets, get most of the attention, the credit markets are much, much larger. These vast markets include everything from 30-year Treasury bonds to securities tied to auto loan financing. In essence, the credit markets act as a vital lubricant throughout the nation's economy, helping businesses to operate and families to purchase a home or pay for college. For instance, home mortgages are often packaged together and resold into the credit markets, and student loan-financing companies use the credit markets to manage their loan-financing business. But in 2008, the credit markets slowed down and in some cases ceased operating as investors grew leery of acquiring debt assets.

When the credit markets falter, the economic effects can be swift and severe, as we've discovered. For instance, auto sales fell off a cliff in October 2008 once it became clear that auto

financing had dried up. Getting approved for home mortgages became much tougher. Credit card interest rates jumped.
Indeed, the credit problems, by making it harder to purchase
goods or expand businesses, were a chief reason many developed economies slid into recession in 2007 and 2008. Businesses
found themselves especially crimped by the credit crunch. Borrowing to pay for acquisitions, the hiring of new employees or
the building of new infrastructure became exceedingly tough,
causing a sharp slowdown in business activity.

A big part of the problem is that an enormous amount of
borrowed money flowed into the credit markets from banks,
hedge funds and cash-rich nations such as China and Japan in
the years before the crisis. For a time, gains made by investing
this borrowed money further amplified the profits financial
firms such as Lehman Brothers, AIG, Goldman Sachs and
others reaped from mortgage-backed securities.

But when those strategies went awry—such as when homeowners stopped being able to pay their mortgages, leading
many mortgage securities to tumble in value—the borrowed
money acted like fuel on a burning building, with debt obligations spiraling out of control. The ensuing failures have made
credit market participants more fearful.

Like the stock markets, the credit markets run on confidence. Buyers of debt are in essence lenders, and they expect to
be paid back, with interest. Thus, when an investor buys Treasury bills from the government, she is essentially loaning the
government money. The government pays her back the amount
she lent, plus interest. Companies do the same thing to raise

debt. When companies fail and debts go unpaid, lenders get nervous. In usual circumstances, the lenders will simply charge higher rates and set tougher conditions for loans. But in the summer and fall of 2008, banks and others became wary about lending anything at all. Like an engine with no oil, the credit markets seized up. For instance, Bank of America decided not to lend to a Chicago window manufacturer in the fall of 2008 and the factory shut its doors in December 2008, laying off 250 workers. After workers protested, Bank of America agreed to extend credit to the firm. Many companies, large and small, have grappled with similar problems during the credit crunch. Another way the credit crunch strikes is in the financing of regular corporate operations, such as payroll and short-term purchases. A lot of this money comes from relatively cheap, short-term loans. When a company can't access such loans because of a credit crunch, it must find other, more expensive ways to finance its business, such as incurring long-term debt or even selling stock to raise funds. Since financing of operations becomes more expensive, companies have fewer funds to invest in new projects or hire new workers.

In the fall of 2008, the credit crunch led to large layoffs and other radical actions as companies grappled with the higher costs of doing business. Citigroup cut 50,000 jobs. General Motors and Ford shuttered plants. Cisco Systems closed its operations for five days to reduce inventory. In November, the economy lost 533,000 non-farm payroll jobs, the worst such loss since 1974.

For individual investors, the credit market crisis became

more than a spectator sport. Many investors, especially those close to retirement or in retirement, held credit investments, usually in the form of Treasurys, corporate bonds or bond mutual funds. Treasurys are usually considered extremely safe, while corporate bonds range from pretty safe to frighteningly risky. Investors who own Treasurys or invest in municipal bonds find themselves getting extremely low interest rate payments, making it challenging to build a nest egg.

The credit crunch was most visibly illuminated when the most widely used bank-to-bank lending rate, the London Interbank Offered Rate (LIBOR), rose sharply during the summer of 2008, negatively affecting credit card interest rates and adjustable-rate mortgages, further harming the economy.

Given the existing credit conditions, banks and others in need of short-term financing continued to suffer and, in some cases, failed altogether. In July 2008, IndyMac Federal Bank, a huge mortgage issuer in California, collapsed, giving the U.S. its own echo of the Northern Rock debacle in the U.K. It marked the second biggest bank failure after Continental Illinois National Bank and Trust Company in 1984, and IndyMac depositors engaged in a minirun before federal insurers assured them that their funds were accounted for. Some depositors had more cash in IndyMac than FDIC insurance covered ($100,000 at the time), creating more angst among individual investors and a race to figure out what was safe. In the case of such a bank failure, insured individual deposits are moved to a healthier institution, where individuals can then access their funds.

LIBOR

LIBOR is the London Interbank Offered Rate, a measure of the rate banks charge one another to lend out money. This obscure term (pronounced LIE-bore) became a star of the credit crisis since it essentially measures the confidence banks have in one another.

Like a thermometer in an ailing child's mouth, LIBOR began to rise disturbingly in early 2008. The rate had fluctuated a bit in 2007 in the wake of the collapse of Northern Rock, but it started an inexorable move higher about one year later. As the rate continued to climb to unseen levels, it became clear that the banking system faced a tremendous and growing crisis. For a time, discussion of LIBOR competed with talk of the Dow Jones Industrial Average.

LIBOR is calculated in a range of ways over a range of time periods, but those time periods are generally quite short. LIBOR can also have an impact on the rates banks charge for credit cards or mortgages.

During the summer of 2008, questions swirled around the huge mortgage players Fannie Mae and Freddie Mac. Would they fail? Would they survive? Would the government save these so-called government-sponsored enterprises? The fate of Fannie and Freddie stood at center stage as the blame game really got under way. The traditional view held that this terrible credit crisis, which would quickly evolve into a global financial crisis, stemmed from a lack of regulation.

True enough, many of the instruments at the heart of the financial problems involved derivatives, which are not regulated in the same fashion as stocks and bonds. At the same time, real estate regulations that determine who is qualified to purchase a home, which are farther up the food chain, were not exactly enforced. But the idea that the George W. Bush years were a period of lax regulation is hard to square with the facts: after Enron collapsed, the Sarbanes-Oxley Act imposed a wide range of new rules on companies and corporate accountants. The crusades of then New York Attorney General Eliot Spitzer were also a form of increased regulation, though, given his position, they usually took the form of lawsuits and settlements. Mr. Spitzer remade Wall Street research, mutual fund trading and the selling of various forms of insurance. The problem was, neither Sarbanes-Oxley nor Spitzer's crusade had a noticeable effect on the actions of Wall Street, especially in the derivatives market.

THE SARBANES-OXLEY ACT

In the wake of the market downturn in 2000 and 2001, several companies failed because of accounting irregularities, most notably the energy trader Enron and the telecom giant WorldCom. These irregularities resulted in criminal convictions for some executives and lost fortunes for investors in and employees of these companies. Reacting to investors' anger about corporate malfeasance, Congress passed the Sarbanes-Oxley Act.

This new regulation increased both oversight of the public accounting firms that oversee publicly traded companies' balance sheets and the amount of regulation of publicly traded companies.

Among the new rules, chief executive officers had to certify the authenticity of financial statements, and a series of new oversight and internal checks and balances were implemented.

Many public companies complained that Sarbanes-Oxley, named for Sen. Paul Sarbanes (D–Md.) and Rep. Michael Oxley (R–Ohio), was too onerous because it required a great deal more paperwork and the establishment of more intensive internal control mechanisms, which usually meant hiring more lawyers or accountants. Many companies that went private during the years after Sarbanes-Oxley was implemented cited the new rules as a reason for leaving the public markets. As initial public offerings grew more dramatically in London and Hong Kong than in New York, critics pointed at Sarbanes-Oxley, sometimes called Sarbox, as a reason for this shift.

Backers of the new rules said the tighter internal controls and accounting industry oversight helped create a stronger, more transparent public marketplace for U.S. companies. A February 2008 survey by BDO Seidman, an accounting firm, found that 65% of technology company chief financial officers said the Sarbanes-Oxley rules related to improved controls and processes had strengthened their company. Some efforts were made on Capitol Hill to curtail Sarbanes-Oxley, but ultimately they failed.

While debate about greater regulation of the derivatives markets came and went both within the marketplace and in Congressional hearings, Washington for the most part let this market grow unimpeded. Others, notably *The Wall Street Journal* editorial page, argued that actions by the government itself had caused the crisis, primarily by encouraging Fannie Mae and Freddie Mac to acquire and fund mortgages for people who couldn't afford them. In other words, it had provided the gasoline for the explosion in subprime debt at the heart of the crisis. There's no question that Fannie and Freddie participated in the lower end of the mortgage market in a risky manner, ultimately putting their own survival at stake. But pinning the entire global financial crisis on Fannie and Freddie seems extreme.

In the end, it was a combination of many things that led to the financial crisis. Far too much borrowing fed into a system predicated on a faulty notion—that real estate prices would always rise, even if just a little. Fannie and Freddie played their part, but so did the Wall Street banks that concocted investment instruments that would turn toxic. And banks, with their lax lending rules, helped fuel the excess to an unimaginable level. Greed took hold, and the large, early real estate–related gains fed a mania that grew into a bubble that burst with terrible results.

FAQ

Why did the crisis take a relatively long time to unfold?

There are several reasons, chief among them the resilient optimism of the crisis's victims. Many firms, including Lehman Brothers, Merrill Lynch and Bear Stearns, believed that things would soon get better and avoided taking steps to address capital shortfalls or other problems. Also, banks such as Washington Mutual and Indy-Mac held out hope that real estate prices would at least bottom if not start to rise again. This didn't happen, and the surprising weakness in real estate prices, especially residential home values, played the key role in driving the crisis from bad to worse.

Should the government have done more to protect investors sooner?

At this point, with the government on the hook for well over $1 trillion in various forms of assistance, it's hard to argue that it could have done more. From the start, the government worked to create solutions that would stave off deeper problems. But each solution—more creative lending rules, an exaggerated definition of "What is a bank?," programs to take toxic debt as collateral—didn't seem to work. That's because the problem, fueled by bor-

FAQ

rowed money, has become too big for one, two or even more small programs to fix.

Why did stock prices sometimes rise sharply in the midst of the credit crunch?

These two markets often have different outlooks, even if examining the same subject. Credit markets tend to attract dour, pessimistic types, while stock investors are an eternally optimistic lot, for the most part. This is because credit markets are dealing with the humdrum notion of having a debt repaid, whereas stock markets are focused on the more dazzling prospects of growth and future success. During the crunch, the credit markets could only be filled with distrust and fear. Stock investors, however, could sometimes get carried away with the notion that the worst had passed. Stock prices were extraordinarily volatile during the height of the crisis in September and October. But in the end, the stock prices reflected the steadfastly grim outlook of the credit markets.

What's the right amount of debt, or leverage, for the financial system?

This is the zillion-dollar question. Most people would argue that whatever the right amount is, we had far too

FAQ

much of it. A similar debt explosion fueled the speculation ahead of the 1929 stock market crash. Banking regulators and others are likely to tweak capital requirements and take additional steps to reduce the amount of leverage, or borrowing, in the system. This great "deleveraging"— essentially the paying down or reduction of debt held by individuals, corporations and investors—is one reason the economy is going through a recession.

Will there still be a subprime debt market?
Of course, and there's one today. It's smaller than it used to be and focused more on credit cards and payday loans as opposed to homes and mortgages. Since lenders can get such high interest rates from those with bad credit, there will always be those who seek to exploit the subprime market. The government could add a lot of new regulations, but that would probably eliminate the subprime market and drive distressed borrowers into more problematic borrowing situations, such as loan sharks and payday loans, which charge even higher rates than subprime loans.

FAQ

What will be the biggest changes in the housing market?

For starters, mortgages of all stripes are and will be much harder to get. After having lent to anyone, banks have suddenly become quite schoolmarmish about doling out mortgages or other loans, taking a very sharp look at a borrower's qualifications. Also, home-value appraisers will rediscover skepticism. In the past, the refinancing boom relied on rather slapdash appraisals, to put it mildly. This practice will go quiet for some time. Last, it will remain a buyer's market for a while. Supply overhangs in nearly all parts of the country will take time to work off. Even tiny Muscatine, Iowa, south of the Quad Cities, reports plenty of new, unsold inventory and more undeveloped inventory. That's the case nearly everywhere in the nation.

FOUR

TSUNAMI

SEPTEMBER 2008 OPENED WITH a presidential campaign in full roar and the financial markets grappling for a handhold. What had seemed like a very troubled market, housing and banking situation in midsummer as banks failed and foreclosures rose had grown dramatically worse. Credit tightness persisted despite central banks around the world injecting hundreds of billions of dollars into the system. Lenders moved warily, fretting that anybody could face failure.

In the markets, attention refocused on the government-sponsored lenders Fannie Mae and Freddie Mac. Stock players had grown convinced that the two mortgage giants at the epicenter of the real estate and subprime crisis could not survive on their own. The share prices of the two firms plunged to near zero. A few weeks earlier, Congress had given U.S. Treasury

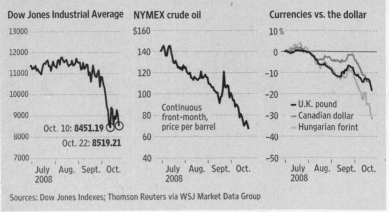

The Globe Churns

Stock, currency and commodity markets signaled that investors believe tougher times are ahead.

Dow Jones Industrial Average

13000
12000
11000
10000
9000
Oct. 10: **8451.19**
8000
Oct. 22: **8519.21**
7000

July Aug. Sept. Oct.
2008

NYMEX crude oil

$160
140
120
100
80 Continuous front-month, price per barrel
60
40

July Aug. Sept. Oct.
2008

Currencies vs. the dollar

10 %
0
-10
-20
-30 ▬ U.K. pound
  ▬ Canadian dollar
  ▬ Hungarian forint
-40
-50

July Aug. Sept. Oct.
2008

Sources: Dow Jones Indexes; Thomson Reuters via WSJ Market Data Group

Secretary Henry Paulson the power and authority to take over Freddie and Fannie if necessary. It came to that far more quickly than anybody expected.

One week after IndyMac had started to fail, Mr. Paulson stepped in and led a government takeover of placed Fannie and Freddie, meaning that the government's implied backing of the two firms had become a reality. Mr. Paulson, along with Federal Reserve chief Ben Bernanke and New York Fed boss Timothy Geithner, would play an instrumental role throughout the crisis, trying all manner of creative solutions.

In essence, Fannie and Freddie became part of the U.S. government, with taxpayers taking on all the liabilities associated with the two firms. That meant that all at once, the U.S. government was on the hook for more than $5 trillion in mortgages.

HENRY PAULSON

When Henry Paulson became President George W. Bush's Treasury secretary in the summer of 2006, a lot of people expressed surprise. At the time, Mr. Paulson was the head of Goldman Sachs, arguably the most powerful investment bank in the world. As its chief, Paulson raked in $37 million in compensation in 2005. As Treasury secretary, he makes $192,000 a year. Talk about a pay cut.

Mr. Paulson's arrival came when President Bush's approval was shrinking and on the eve of the Democratic Party victories in the 2006 congressional elections. Washington insiders didn't think Paulson would get much done in the remaining two years of a Bush administration, especially with Democrats controlling the Senate and the House. Of course, events showed otherwise when Mr. Paulson was thrust into the limelight to do battle with the financial crisis, which showed few signs of abating as he left his position.

All of Mr. Paulson's fiery, combative personality has been on display during the crisis. But he's also shown a softer side, getting down on one knee to beg House Speaker Nancy Pelosi to help pass the Treasury's $700 billion rescue package in the fall of 2008. His role in the bailout has also been what Hollywood would term "against type." A ferocious free marketer, he has often talked about how much he hates having to rescue his former colleagues and competitors on Wall Street.

Mr. Paulson was a star football player at Dartmouth and worked at the Pentagon and in the White House during the Richard Nixon administration before joining Goldman Sachs in 1974. He quickly rose through Goldman's investment banking division, taking over the firm in 1999 after his co-CEO Jon Corzine was forced out of the firm. Mr. Corzine, a Democrat, eventually became a U.S. Senator representing New Jersey and is now the Governor of New Jersey. (Goldman has a long pedigree of prepping people for government service in both parties.)

Mr. Paulson is an environmental advocate and served as chairman of the Nature Conservancy, which works on land preservation, sometimes by acquiring the land itself and keeping it from development. He is an outdoorsman, having canoed and camped in the Boundary Waters Canoe Area Wilderness in northern Minnesota.

In the third quarter of 2008, Fannie reported a loss of $29 billion amid mortgage bets gone bad and said it needed more government cash to keep operating. Freddie fared little better.

The takeover of Fannie and Freddie sent a chill through the marketplace. Though the giants had implied government backing, the actual takeover implied something altogether different: that things had gotten very bad. And they would quickly get worse.

In the two weeks after the Fannie and Freddie takeover, the credit spreads got worse. These spreads calculate the difference between interest rates paid by U.S. Treasury's and other kinds of nongovernment debt. The wider the spread between supersafe U.S. debt and riskier nongovernment debt, the higher the level of concern or fear in the marketplace. A common measure of such fear is the so-called TED spread, which measures the difference between interest rates on three-month Treasury bills and the three-month rate banks charge one another to lend to each other. (TED is short for "Treasury" and "ED," or Eurodollar futures, an interbank lending instrument.) In mid-September 2008, the TED spread broke its previous record, set during the 1987 stock market crash. It rose even higher in early October 2008.

The rising credit spreads made borrowing exceedingly difficult or, in the best cases, incredibly expensive. This caused problems for all sorts of companies dependent on credit, ranging from banks to electronics retailers and even to entire countries facing severe debt problems. The credit market problems created severe situations for the financial firms, many of which had been riding very high just a few years previously.

Those in the bull's-eye included Morgan Stanley, a venerable firm descended from the House of Morgan; Lehman Brothers, once cotton merchants who had begun work in Alabama before the Civil War; Merrill Lynch, the thundering herd with the largest brokerage network in the country; and AIG, a global insurance titan that had started by selling life insurance in Shanghai to the Chinese.

Lehman Brothers would kick off the course of events, and its demise remains hotly debated today. By Friday, September 12, it became clear that Lehman could not survive. Much like Bear Stearns in the spring, Lehman had suffered a vicious run, fed by its weak, real estate–heavy balance sheet. Even though

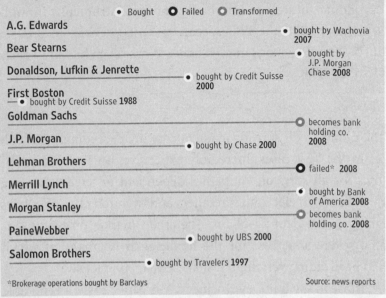

End of the Line

The transformation of Goldman Sachs and Morgan Stanley into traditional bank holding companies marks the end of Wall Street's big standalone investment banks.

● Bought   ◉ Failed   ◎ Transformed

A.G. Edwards — ● bought by Wachovia 2007

Bear Stearns — ● bought by J.P. Morgan Chase 2008

Donaldson, Lufkin & Jenrette — ● bought by Credit Suisse 2000

First Boston — ● bought by Credit Suisse 1988

Goldman Sachs — ◎ becomes bank holding co. 2008

J.P. Morgan — ● bought by Chase 2000

Lehman Brothers — ◉ failed* 2008

Merrill Lynch — ● bought by Bank of America 2008

Morgan Stanley — ◎ becomes bank holding co. 2008

PaineWebber — ● bought by UBS 2000

Salomon Brothers — ● bought by Travelers 1997

*Brokerage operations bought by Barclays

Source: news reports

Lehman had known it was vulnerable for more than a year, the company's tenacious CEO, Richard Fuld, believed that Lehman, so often viewed as a potential takeover target, could weather the storm once more. But his stubbornness prevented Lehman from selling assets, such as its Neuberger Berman money-management arm, in a timely manner in order to raise badly needed capital to offset its large real estate–related losses. Instead, Mr. Fuld bet on real estate values' improving—not a shrewd bet in the end.

LEHMAN BROTHERS

When Lehman died, many people started talking about its long, storied history. Indeed, Lehman did start a long time ago, back in 1850, as an Alabama cotton merchant. The German brothers who founded the firm followed the cotton market to New York City in 1858 and continued to expand its franchise to include stock underwriting.

Lehman did a lot of work with Goldman Sachs in the early part of the 20th century, and a Lehman ran the firm until 1969, when Robert Lehman died. Not long after that, Lehman fell on difficult times and was eventually acquired by American Express in 1984, becoming part of Shearson Lehman. After the 1987 stock market crash, the firm expanded to become Shearson Lehman Hutton.

New management at American Express led to Lehman's spin-off in 1994. From its beginnings as a newly independent company, Lehman was frequently the target of takeover speculation. But CEO Dick Fuld kept the predators at bay and steadily expanded the business to include a larger asset-management arm.

The firm had a strong reputation in the bond market and played especially aggressively in the mortgage market. Indeed, its voracious appetite for mortgage-related business, in both commercial and residential markets, led directly to its demise in the fall of 2008. The day after Lehman failed, the government stepped in to rescue the insurance giant AIG.

With investors taking their assets out of Lehman, and other Wall Street firms and hedge funds refusing to trade with the firm, Lehman faced what had become common on Wall Street: the long weekend, usually set at the New York Fed's office in lower Manhattan. Long-Term Capital Management, the failed hedge fund whose travails were detailed earlier in the book, had met there for its rescue. Bear Stearns had sought its salvation in the same stone temple. It was now Lehman's turn. Bankers, lawyers and others gathered to discuss the fate of the firm. Starting on Friday, the negotiators generally have until Sunday evening, when the Asian markets open.

Flashback to March 2008, when Bear Stearns faced extinction. In this case, regulators were eager to prevent its failure, fearing widespread systemic problems. This was early on in the crisis, and Bear, as a large broker to hedge funds and other traders in complex products, may not have been too big to fail, but it was considered too complex. Thus, the Fed stepped in to guarantee questionable debts held by Bear Stearns in order to get J.P. Morgan to acquire the company. Some critics argue that if Lehman had faced failure in the spring of 2008, as Bear had, it might have found regulators more willing to rescue it.

On the weekend of September 13 and 14, regulators felt they'd learned a great deal about the unfolding credit crisis in the months after the rescue of Bear. Indeed, rightly or wrongly, they felt some confidence that they could let Lehman Brothers fail without causing too much of a wider crisis. Thus, they were less willing to lend a hand, as they had in Bear's case, to help Lehman and potential bidders, notably Bank of America and Barclays Bank of the U.K., to forge a possible deal over the weekend. As the various parties fenced, it became clear that Lehman would not be rescued. Bidders decided that Lehman's bits could be more easily—and cheaply—acquired through bankruptcy proceedings. And regulators, including the Federal Reserve, the Securities and Exchange Commission and the Treasury, made it clear that they would move things quickly through such proceedings, ideally mitigating the impact of Lehman's liquidation. Those choices meant one thing: Lehman Brothers would liquidate on Monday morning. The firm's failure added to the more than 80,000 financial jobs lost since the crisis struck in 2007, many of them in the New York area, where Lehman was based.

As Lehman faced its bankruptcy filing, Merrill Lynch found itself in an only modestly better position. Bank of America had edged away from the Lehman talks to find that Merrill was also looking to find a buyer. Though not nearly as unhealthy as Lehman, Merrill believed that a Lehman failure would leave it vulnerable to the negative views of short sellers and a fall in confidence that would make operating increasingly difficult. It didn't want to test that scenario, so on Monday, September 15, its officers agreed to an all-stock $50 billion takeover by Bank of America. Bank of America's shares fell in the weeks following the deal, reducing the takeover price.

Combining the two firms would create a banking and investment banking powerhouse. Though much of Merrill Lynch's brokerage business would remain intact, the combining of the investment banking divisions of the two companies would eventually lead to large job losses. In addition, the duplication of back-office and other support functions would reduce the number of jobs at the combined company.

More starkly, Merrill's new owners didn't hail from Wall

MERRILL LYNCH

Merrill Lynch's famous bull will still traipse through fine china shops and open fields in the future, but the bull is now owned by a North Carolina bank. Like other Wall Street firms that collapsed, Merrill found itself holding far too many toxic assets to survive to fight another day. But instead of an outright collapse, it engineered a quick sale to Bank of America, one of the world's biggest banks.

Unlike other Wall Street firms that failed, Merrill Lynch had an enormous business serving individual investors through its brokerage arm. That business made Merrill a household name and probably helped it avoid a darker fate.

Charles Merrill started the firm in 1914, adding partner Edmund Lynch to the nameplate in 1915. The company initially made its name as an investor, for instance backing the vast expansion of the Safeway grocery store chain in the 1920s and 1930s. It began to build its large brokerage business, primarily through acquisitions in the 1940s, and was known for some time by the ungainly Merrill Lynch, Pierce, Fenner & Smith. That name survived on official exchange memberships and other areas, but eventually the company simplified its corporate name to Merrill Lynch & Co.

On the Street during the 1980s and 1990s, Merrill always seemed to trail behind its tonier competitors, notably Goldman Sachs and Morgan Stanley. This changed to a degree under E. Stanley O'Neal, who took over the firm in 2001. Mr. O'Neal cut staff and aggressively expanded Merrill's private-equity investing and mortgage-related businesses.

This worked well for some time as Merrill made record profits and Mr. O'Neal received gaudy compensation packages. But Merrill found itself ill prepared for the subprime mortgage crisis, adding to its holdings even after it became clear that strategy had run aground. Mr. O'Neal was tossed in favor of John Thain, an ex-Goldman executive and former head of the New York Stock Exchange. Mr. Thain tried for more than a year to save the firm, but the bad debts proved too big a burden, leading to the sale.

Street or even Midtown Manhattan. The new bosses lived in Charlotte, N.C. Wall Street was steadily disappearing into the maw of the financial crisis.

Contrary to the expectations of regulators, the news of Lehman's failure jolted the markets and marked the moment when the credit crunch became the global financial crisis. Share prices plunged everywhere except in much of Asia, where many of the markets were closed because of holidays. European shares skidded 4%, and the Dow Jones Industrial Average fell in similar fashion. By the end of the day, investors and policy makers had already started questioning the wisdom of letting Lehman go bust. But the bailout police at the Federal Reserve and the Treasury, led by Ben Bernanke, New York Fed chief Timothy Geithner and Treasury Secretary Henry Paulson, had little time to answer. Knocking at the government door looking for a rescue was AIG, the titanic insurance company with tentacles into every nook and cranny of Wall Street and the broader global financial markets.

AIG is known primarily as an insurance company, but it had really evolved into a complex financial services firm. It had a reputation for trading just about anything: credit-default swaps, specifically tailored investment vehicles, all manners of commodities. Its woes, similar to those of all the other companies in trouble, stemmed from bad real estate bets and an excessive amount of borrowing that amplified its losses. One day the regulators let Lehman fail, the next they threw AIG a lifeline with a $20 billion loan. That figure soon grew to $85 billion, and by year-end AIG would take $150 billion in government loans and aid in order to remain afloat.

AIG

AIG rose from humble beginnings as the American International Group in Shanghai, China, to become one of the largest and most powerful insurance companies in the world. Its history, which starts in 1919 with the China office, is encapsulated in two smart, aggressive and clever people: Cornelius Vander Starr, its founder, and Maurice "Hank" Greenberg, his successor.

Mr. Vander Starr was the first Westerner allowed to sell insurance to the Chinese, and he quickly expanded his business around the globe. Though he did well elsewhere, his U.S. businesses struggled until Mr. Greenberg took them over in 1962. Mr. Vander Starr made Mr. Greenberg his successor in 1968.

A World War II and Korean War veteran, Mr. Greenberg turned AIG into a complex financial juggernaut. Critics complained that it was difficult to decipher how AIG made its princely profits. Mr. Greenberg, however, brooked no criticism, ruling his firm with an iron fist and enormous energy. He once barked sharply back at a group of clergy during an annual meeting when they questioned him about diversity efforts at AIG.

Mr. Greenberg's hard-charging ways eventually led him into conflict with then New York Attorney General Eliot Spitzer in

2005. Mr. Spitzer's investigation into insurance sales and derivatives eventually led to Mr. Greenberg's ouster in 2005. Mr. Greenberg's two successors struggled to match Mr. Greenberg's performance.

As the financial crisis unfolded, AIG found itself holding enormous losses. The government stepped in to rescue AIG, and within two months of the rescue, the company had already required $150 billion in aid to continue operating. Despite its travails, AIG can still be seen on the front of the jerseys of the Manchester United soccer team, the richest sports club in the world.

On Tuesday, September 16, the Asian markets finally opened and share prices plunged, with Japan down more than 4%. Shares in Europe and the U.S. followed suit. It became clear that the financial system faced a full-blown crisis. Morgan Stanley and Wachovia shares plunged. Morgan Stanley, trading near $90 a share in early 2007, saw the price plunge below $10 a share. Wachovia fell from the $50 range to single digits in a similar time frame.

Wachovia had a special set of difficulties. One of the nation's largest banks, also based in Charlotte, N.C., it had made an ill-timed purchase of Golden West Financial, a California-based bank that specialized in exotic mortgage lending. The acquisition, in 2006, came just as the California real estate market started to dip, saddling Wachovia with an enormous amount of bad debt.

In the chaotic, merry-go-round antics of those September days, Morgan Stanley and Wachovia talked about a possible combination. Nothing came of these talks, and soon Wachovia started chatting up Citigroup. Not long after, one more government-sweetened deal was announced, with Citigroup taking over Wachovia, backed by Federal Reserve loan guarantees for Wachovia's lousiest assets. But Wells Fargo, a San Francisco bank less stung by those banks clustered around Wall Street, emerged to make a non-government-aided bid for Wachovia. After a bit of bickering, Citigroup acquiesced and Wells Fargo won the day.

Morgan Stanley, meantime, laid all its chips on the Japanese. Specifically, it negotiated over a three-week period into mid-October before securing a $9 billion investment from Mitsubishi UFJ Financial Group. During this period, Morgan Stanley's shares gyrated as it fluttered between life and death. The final terms of the deal heavily favored the Japanese bank, but the capital lifeline gave Morgan Stanley the chance to survive, if barely.

MORGAN STANLEY

Morgan Stanley was born in 1935 after the Glass-Steagall law passed, making it illegal for banks to own investment banks. That meant the famed House of Morgan, J.P. Morgan & Co., had to split into two firms: J.P. Morgan the bank and Morgan Stanley the investment bank.

The new investment bank quickly became a major player in the space, drawing on its strong pedigree to establish a reputation as the toniest white-shoe banking firm on Wall Street. During its early decades it led numerous high-profile offerings from venerable American companies such as General Motors, IBM and AT&T.

During the 1980s and 1990s, Morgan Stanley, along with Goldman Sachs, dominated much of the investment banking business. Morgan Stanley also expanded by acquiring Van Kampen Funds, the brokerage firm Dean Witter and the Discover credit card company. Old hands fretted that this expansion was watering down the pure Morgan blood that had originally coursed through the firm's veins.

In the summer of 2005, a revolt against CEO Philip Purcell, led primarily by the old hands, eventually led to Mr. Purcell's retirement. He was succeeded by John Mack who still runs the firm.

Along with Goldman Sachs, Morgan Stanley has thus far survived the financial crisis. It has sold Discover and taken in a big investment from Bank of Tokyo–Mitsubishi UFJ of Japan. Its shares have struggled, and several times, investors have expected it to fall into the arms of a larger bank. Like Goldman, it converted to a bank holding company in September 2008, leaving no major U.S. investment banks behind.

In the midst of the negotiations, and just one week after Lehman Brothers disappeared and Merrill Lynch agreed to the Bank of America takeover, Goldman and Morgan Stanley registered as bank holding companies, essentially ending the era of the big U.S. investment bank.

By becoming bank holding companies, the two firms acknowledged the obvious: they needed to reduce their high-flying borrowing, they needed more capital and they would

BANK HOLDING COMPANY
VS. INVESTMENT BANK

Following the Depression-era implementation of the Glass-Steagall Act in 1933, which came about in response to the 1929 stock market crash and the subsequent failure of many banks, banks were divided into two basic entities: bank holding companies and investment banks. Bank holding companies, essentially commercial banks, fell under the regulatory purview of the Federal Reserve System. Investment banks were regulated primarily by the Securities and Exchange Commission. Under Glass-Steagall, bank holding companies and investment banks had to operate as separate and distinct companies. This led to the breakup of J.P. Morgan into J.P. Morgan the bank and Morgan Stanley the investment bank.

A series of mergers in the 1980s and 1990s steadily whittled away the separation of banks and investment banks and in 1999, the Gramm-Leach-Bliley Act effectively repealed Glass-Steagall restrictions on banks and investment banks operating under the same roof. This bill essentially recognized the facts on the ground, since Citibank had already acquired an investment banking arm in 1998. Today, Bank of America, J.P. Morgan, Deutsche Bank, UBS and other banks all have large investment banking operations, even though they are bank holding companies.

In the midst of the financial crisis, Morgan Stanley and Goldman Sachs registered as bank holding companies. This meant that they fell under the Fed's regulatory purview, could take in customer deposits and would have easier access to Fed funding and lending. This change in status also meant that Morgan Stanley (and Goldman Sachs) would have to reduce the amount of borrowing, or leverage, they used to make investments on their own behalf.

> **Despite their new official status, Morgan Stanley and Goldman Sachs will continue to operate investment banking units. They will continue to advise on mergers and acquisitions, trade and invest for their own accounts and provide investment advice to clients. But they will operate in this sphere with more oversight and have a lesser ability to take on large, debt-fueled risks.**

come under the regulatory purview of the Federal Reserve. This maneuver would also give the two companies easier access to Federal Reserve funds, considered crucial to survival.

If the week of September 15 led to the radical reshaping of Wall Street, that week would also mark the beginning of a brutal period that brought the viability of the entire global financial system into question. More large failures took place, including the collapse of the nation's largest savings and loan, Washington Mutual, better known as WaMu. J.P. Morgan acquired the bedraggled thrift, beset by bad mortgage debts, for about $2 billion. The combination meant one less bank and thousands more lost jobs.

The takeover stunned Wall Street and spooked regulators, investors, politicians and bankers. The FDIC, which insures cash deposits, did not have enough funds on hand to insure the deposits at the thrift, meaning that without the J.P. Morgan takeover, the FDIC would have become insolvent. Of course, the government can always replenish the FDIC's coffers, but the notion of cash deposits facing widespread danger for the first time since the Great Depression sent a chill throughout the

The Week That Changed American Capitalism

**Dow Jones
Industrial Average**
30-minute ticks

Sept. 2008
Sunday 14th

Monday 15th

Tuesday 16th

THE EVENTS

Sleepless weekend:
Would-be suitors decline
to buy struggling Lehman
Brothers. Merrill Lynch
agrees to sell itself to
Bank of America. Ten big
banks circle their wagons,
creating a $70 billion
borrowing facility.

In sign of broadening crisis,
insurance giant American
International Group—which
issued policies protecting
against corporate defaults
—suffers credit-rating downgrade, and shares plummet.
AIG seeks as much as $70
billion from government.
Lehman files for bankruptcy.

Fearful Investors: Shares
of Reserve Primary Fund
—billed as a super-safe
money-market fund—fall
below $1 a share due to
Lehman exposure. Credit
markets seize up: With
banks fearful of lending,
Libor interbank interest
rates soar.

GOVERNMENT MOVES

Months after brokering
the sale of tottering Bear
Stearns, U.S. government
**rules out a rescue
of 158-year-old Lehman.**

Treasury Secretary Hank
Paulson, asked if the
Lehman failure signaled
an end to federal rescues,
says, **"Don't read it as 'no
more.'"** Behind the
scenes, Fed and Treasury
study an AIG bailout.

**U.S. government seizes
control of AIG in a $85
billion bailout,** an unprecedented bid to contain crisis.
Some global exchanges
suspend trading as prices
plunge. Federal Reserve
keeps key rate unchanged.

Lehman CDS*

Sept. 12
last trade recorded
due to default

AIG's daily share price

Monday

Overnight dollar Libor

Tuesday

*The amount an investor must pay annually for protection against a default on $10 million in debt over five years.
†Daily settlement price on the continuous front-month contract on the Comex division of NYMEX.

The financial storm that began with bad bets on mortgage-backed investments reached new intensity with September's federal takeover of mortgage giants Fannie Mae and Freddie Mac. That historic bailout failed to soothe markets, and shockwaves spread well beyond financial firms and brought unprecedented government interventions.

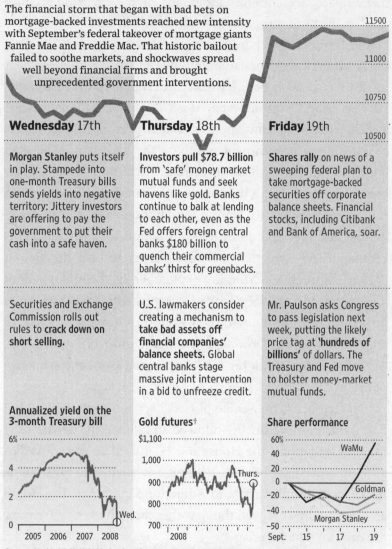

Wednesday 17th

Morgan Stanley puts itself in play. Stampede into one-month Treasury bills sends yields into negative territory: Jittery investors are offering to pay the government to put their cash into a safe haven.

Securities and Exchange Commission rolls out rules to **crack down on short selling.**

Annualized yield on the 3-month Treasury bill

Thursday 18th

Investors pull $78.7 billion from 'safe' money market mutual funds and seek havens like gold. Banks continue to balk at lending to each other, even as the Fed offers foreign central banks $180 billion to quench their commercial banks' thirst for greenbacks.

U.S. lawmakers consider creating a mechanism to **take bad assets off financial companies' balance sheets.** Global central banks stage massive joint intervention in a bid to unfreeze credit.

Gold futures†

Friday 19th

Shares rally on news of a sweeping federal plan to take mortgage-backed securities off corporate balance sheets. Financial stocks, including Citibank and Bank of America, soar.

Mr. Paulson asks Congress to pass legislation next week, putting the likely price tag at **'hundreds of billions'** of dollars. The Treasury and Fed move to bolster money-market mutual funds.

Share performance

Sources: Markit (CDS); WSJ Market Data Group (stocks); British Bankers' Association (Libor); Federal Reserve (3-month Treasury yield); NYMEX via WSJ Market Data Group (gold futures).

marketplace. Searches on Google for "Is my checking account safe" or "Is my savings account safe" skyrocketed.

But the crisis was hardly over. Analysts at many Wall Street firms believed that the large amounts of toxic real estate debt must be dealt with before the credit crunch could ease. Treasury Secretary Paulson prepared a $700 billion bailout package aimed, initially, at removing this toxic debt from balance sheets by having the government purchase the bad debt. (The plan later morphed in several directions, including direct investments into banks.) But the bailout plan ran into stiff opposition in Congress, especially among Republicans. Republican presidential nominee Sen. John McCain famously "suspended" his campaign and went to Washington to try to help the bailout package through. On Monday, September 29, the initial bailout vote failed and stocks dropped sharply, with the Dow Jones Industrial Average plunging 777 points, or just short of 7%, to 10,365. It was the Dow's biggest point drop on record. Mr. McCain's campaign never really recovered from the sequence of events.

On October 1, the Senate passed a version of the bailout bill and the House eventually followed suit. Since the Senate can't initiate legislation—the House must—it used an old trick, digging up a dormant bill and using it as a shell. The bill's name: the Mental Health Parity and Addiction Equity Act. The House also eventually approved the new measure, giving the Treasury the cash to fight the crisis.

Failures spread overseas and underscored the global nature of the crisis. In the U.K., the Spanish bank Banco Santander acquired Bradford & Bingley, a financial services firm, with government help. Dexia, a Belgian lender, received a government bailout. Fortis, a Belgian financial services firm, found itself unable to raise badly needed capital and was eventually acquired by BNP Paribas, the French bank.

By early October, it had become clear that Lehman's failure, among other things, had set off a cavalcade of unexpected events and contributed to a systemic crisis in the financial system. Stock prices plunged, and concerns about the viability of the financial system rose. Governments in Europe, Asia and the U.S. promised to do whatever it took to solve the financial crisis. But some governments had to rescue themselves first.

The starkest example of a nation rocked by the crisis was Iceland. As a member of the European Union, this island nation of about 300,000 people had easy access to individuals across the continent and in the U.K. But as the manager of its own currency, the krona, Iceland often found itself paying higher short-term interest rates than the European Central Bank. Icelandic banks took full advantage of this, offering online savings accounts to yield-hungry customers in the U.K., France, Germany and elsewhere.

Iceland's banks grew dramatically, coming to dominate the Icelandic economy. The assets held on the banks' balance sheets dwarfed the country's GDP. Many of those assets, however, had links to lousy investments, notably real estate in booming property markets in the U.S. and Europe. As the financial crisis worsened, the Icelandic banks found themselves in a tough position. Depositors began withdrawing funds, but soon the Icelandic banks stopped allowing withdrawals. Essentially, the Icelandic banking system collapsed. The government took over nearly all the private banks, and interest rates skyrocketed as Iceland sought to keep money from flowing out of the country.

With its banking system frozen, the island nation watched retail supplies shrink and disappear. Workers from Eastern Europe, no longer working, returned to the continent. Iceland's debt-driven party ended—abruptly. By mid-November, the normally placid Icelanders were rioting and calling for the government to step down.

As Iceland teetered, along with other countries such as Hungary, the credit crisis seemed bent on laying waste to the developed-world economic system. Governments kept trying to find a solution—lower interest rates, central banks pumping money into the system, corporate rescues, government takeovers—but things only seemed to get worse.

In late September and into October, the problems in the financial sector poured out into other parts of the economy. Blue-chip companies, which actively use "commercial paper" to fund day-to-day business activities, found this market suddenly closed. Commercial paper represents short-term loans, sometimes as short as a day, and money market mutual funds invest in this paper. But the credit crunch has forced even this usually routine market into deep crisis.

Blue-chip companies that had difficulty selling commercial paper had to find alternatives to fund their business operations. One reason the commercial paper market stumbled is because of Lehman's collapse. Several money market funds held Lehman commercial paper. When Lehman failed, some of these funds fell below the $1 share price they must always maintain, effectively failing.

The remarkable problems in the commercial paper market forced the government and Federal Reserve to devise a plan to rescue that market as well. Messrs. Paulson, Geithner and Bernanke once again displayed a zealous desire to do almost anything imaginable to help rescue the markets. It seemed, in the wake of the ill-judged decision to let Lehman fail, that the trio of financial medics were prepared to do just about anything. They set up a program to insure money market funds against any possible failure, which most surviving money markets ended up signing up for. This program helped restore some confidence to the commercial paper trading markets, though these markets remained historically weak by year-end.

The approach to mending the credit markets flowed from the common regulatory plan during the financial crisis: throw enough money at the problem, and eventually it will get solved. This was one theory espoused by Fed chief Ben Bernanke in his academic study of the Great Depression. Mr. Bernanke spent much of his academic career studying the causes of the Great Depression, examining what regulators and the government could have done differently in order to avoid that calamity. The Fed, led by Mr. Bernanke, and other regulators has had to draw on that academic expertise, coming up with creative strategies to try and solve the financial crisis. The Fed, for in-

TIMOTHY GEITHNER

Timothy Geithner is the president of the Federal Reserve Bank of New York and the incoming Treasury secretary in the Obama administration. As head of the New York Fed, Mr. Geithner has played an instrumental role in devising the multiple rescue, bailout and liquidity programs the Federal Reserve and the Treasury have implemented to try to solve the financial crisis.

Mr. Geithner, has worked with Fed chief Ben Bernanke and Treasury Secretary Henry Paulson during the crisis, with Mr. Geithner playing a modestly quieter role than his two partners. He is considered very bright and has a calm, diplomatic demeanor. As the head of the New York Fed, he is in the front row in dealing with the troubled banks and securities firms headquartered in New York.

Prior to becoming head of the New York Fed, Mr. Geithner worked in the Clinton administration under Treasury Secretaries Robert Rubin and Lawrence Summers. He has also worked overseas and played a key role in previous financial crises in Asia, Mexico and Brazil. He is a graduate of Dartmouth College.

stance, has lent money against questionable real estate–related assets. It liberalized the definition of a bank to give more companies access to its funds. It bent rules to guarantee funds in previously unguaranteed markets, such as commercial paper.

BEN BERNANKE

Imagine spending all of your life learning how to fly a commercial airplane and then suddenly finding yourself alone in such a plane screaming through the sky. Ha, you'd think, I know how to fly this thing, no problem.

Fantasy? More like Ben Bernanke's reality. Mr. Bernanke, the head of the Federal Reserve, spent most of his academic career studying the Great Depression, its causes and ways it could be prevented in the future. This work has come in quite handy as the U.S. economy—and the global economy along with it—has teetered on the edge of a financial market collapse and the possibility of a Hobbesian recession that could rival the subject of Mr. Bernanke's study.

Mr. Bernanke, like other financial industry titans such as Warren Buffett, has had an interest in finance and economics since childhood. He grew up in Georgia and helped out at his father's drugstore as a teenager. His education is top-flight, with an undergraduate degree from Harvard and a Ph.D. in economics from the Massachusetts Institute of Technology.

He eventually taught at Princeton University, chairing its economic department before beginning his latest stint in public service. He served as Fed governor from 2002 to 2005 and then took a position on the Bush administration's Council of Economic Advisers before getting the nomination to succeed Alan Greenspan as chairman of the Federal Reserve System. He received Senate approval for that job in early 2006 and has been in that role ever since, with his term as chairman set to expire in 2010.

Mr. Bernanke has very quickly proven himself a creative and adaptive Fed chair. This is hardly surprising, given some of his quirkier academic insights. He once said that if the Fed worried about deflation, it could simply toss money from helicopters in order to induce more spending. This earned him the sobriquet "Helicopter Ben," though he has often insisted that this was just a figure of speech to demonstrate the Fed's power to effect change.

He, along with New York Fed chief Tim Geithner, have worked overtime to show all that the Fed can do. It has lent billions to back takeovers in the banking and finance arena. It has pumped AIG, the insurance giant, full of money—and that bet may not work. It has expanded its lending facility to include many other firms besides the banks it oversees. It has even decided to enter the commercial paper market, essentially making short-term loans to any company interested in getting such a loan.

This is just a sampling of the creativity Mr. Bernanke has employed to try to rescue the financial system, the credit markets and the global economy. It does appear that in the near term, his methods may have avoided catastrophe. But in the long term, policy makers are unsure how the cavalcade of bailouts, rescues, imaginative financings and other magical maneuvers will affect the economy. The piper may yet have to be paid in a different way. For now, though, Mr. Bernanke looks like the bearded wise man who can stave off disaster. Even the petulant Nobel Prize winner Paul Krugman, no fan of anything remotely related to President George W. Bush, has praised Mr. Bernanke's efforts. Of course, Mr. Bernanke used to be Mr. Krugman's boss at Princeton.

It helped engineer various takeover deals and intervened in markets in ways it had never done before. All of this, however, didn't prevent the crisis reaching its nadir in October.

As Iceland collapsed, regulators including the Federal Reserve, the International Monetary Fund and the European Central Bank dug deeper. Global interest rates were cut, hundreds of billions in deposits were guaranteed, central banks pumped countless billions into the financial system and new programs were established to facilitate the purchase of securitized loans such as pools of auto loans and credit card debt. All told, policy makers used an "everything *and* the kitchen sink" strategy to take the financial system away from the abyss. Part of that kitchen sink strategy included the partial nationalization of banks, which got under way in the U.K. first, with the U.S. and others following soon after. This strategy took a page from Sweden's handling of its banking collapse in the early 1990s. After the nationalization stabilized the banking system, Sweden reprivatized its banks.

The coordinated effort to invest directly in banks, providing them with badly needed funds, seemed to lessen the fear of outright systemic collapse, though severe problems remained. Like a test pilot in a multifaceted terrible situation, regulators had managed to figure out how to start the engine, but the plane still needed a lot more power and continued to spin toward the ground.

In the fall of 2008, the government unveiled several plans to try to rescue the system. It had deployed nearly half of the $700 billion Troubled Assets Relief Program (TARP) funds. It had

A New Set of Tools

Major elements of the federal government's expanded response to the financial crisis

TREASURY will:

■ Use up to $250 billion from the $700 billion financial rescue package to purchase senior preferred shares in banks. In addition to the nine banks at right, thousands of others may participate

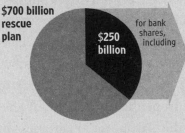

$700 billion rescue plan

$250 billion for bank shares, including

Value of shares, in billions

Bank of America $25

J.P. Morgan Chase 25

Citigroup 25

Wells Fargo 25

Goldman Sachs 10

Morgan Stanley 10

Bank of N.Y. Mellon 3

State Street 2

FDIC will:

■ Guarantee 100% of newly issued senior unsecured debt of banks, thrifts and some holding companies for three years

■ Provide unlimited deposit insurance for bank accounts used by small businesses through Dec. 31, 2009

FEDERAL RESERVE will:

■ Buy high-quality, three-month maturity commercial paper through April 30, 2009, backstopping a market used by major corporations to pay for day-to-day operations

BANKS involved will:

■ Issue preferred stock carrying a 5% annual dividend, rising to 9% after five years

■ Face caps on executive compensation, restrictions on dividend payments and more pressure to help homeowners and to lend money

Source: U.S. Treasury Dept.

pledged $600 billion to purchase mortgage-backed securities backed by Fannie Mae and Freddie Mac. It established a commercial paper lending facility that could eventually top $1 trillion. It had backed hundreds of billions in FDIC-backed debt. Even with all of these funds focused on solving the crisis, questions about the efficacy of the rescue haunted the market and the credit crunch persisted. By the end of 2008, the government had pledged more than $7 trillion in various loans and guarantees to try and solve the financial crisis.

On top of the financial problems, other economic crises grabbed the government's attention. The Big Three automakers worked Congress and the White House for their own bailout program. And states, beset by rapidly dwindling tax receipts, also asked for aid. The financial tsunami had spread deeply into the so-called real economy, with the prospect of deep recession and large job losses on the horizon.

FAQ

Why has the government spent so much money rescuing financial firms?

Policy makers believed that allowing these firms to fail would have created severe problems for the financial system, up to and including outright collapse. In fact, many feared during the early part of October 2008 that the financial system would collapse under the weight of enormous real estate–related debts gone bad. Such a collapse would have meant massive bank failures, a sharp fall in economic growth and millions of lost jobs. It also would've provided a very large challenge: putting it all back together again so that banks could lend and people could invest. The collapse of the financial system would almost certainly lead to economic disaster in a manner similar to or greater than that of the Great Depression. Government officials believed that the steps they took made such a scenario far less likely.

It seemed as if the government made all this up as it went along. Is that true?

Well, in a way, yes. The combination of problems and the enormity of the crisis made traditional tactics in a tough economy, such as raising or lowering interest rates, seem like BB guns at a gunfight. Thus, government officials did, in fact, have to make things up as they went along. The

FAQ

Federal Reserve became extremely creative about how it would use its balance sheet. The Treasury, underscoring the unprecedented nature of the situation, changed its mind at least once about how best to use the $700 billion rescue program to rescue the economy.

What other parts of the world have been and will be affected by the crisis?

Nearly every country has been affected. Some places, such as Iceland and Hungary, face severe issues, primarily because of bad bank borrowing and investing coming home to overwhelm the local economy. Other countries, such as Ireland and Spain, face problems from collapsing property markets. The U.K., with falling home values and carnage in its financial sector, is expected to face a deeper downturn than other major European countries. Ironically, the U.K. seemed to have led the way out of the crisis with its decision to invest directly in its troubled banks, a move quickly followed by other European Union countries and the U.S. Russia, like the U.K., has faced a double whammy: its banks face exposure to bad debt, and the plunge in oil prices, a main source of its revenue, has also stung. Its stock market has fallen dramatically and has frequently had to close in order to restore order. Eastern Europe and most emerging economies also face difficul-

FAQ

ties stemming from the financial crisis, either because of greater difficulty borrowing money or because of economic downturns in key export markets.

Who will be best off after the crisis?
China seems to be in decent shape so far, though its growth rate has slowed and it remains extremely dependent on exports to the U.S. and other countries to keep growing. If the U.S. consumer takes a breather, that will have negative repercussions for China. Brazil, with its diverse economy, is in better shape than its neighbors, especially oil-dependent Venezuela and the fiscal basket case Argentina. Japan, whose banks did not participate heavily in the real estate–related debt shenanigans, ought to be safer than most. But because it still relies heavily on exports for growth, its stock market has suffered harshly during the crisis. One other reason Japan's market has suffered: it has remained liquid and open, meaning that those who are forced to sell securities in order to repay redemptions find Japan one of the few places they can do so.

When will it end?
It seems that the worst of the credit crunch is past, but it could return if government-led efforts fail to spark more bank lending. With systemic risk seemingly out of the

FAQ

way, policy makers can focus on trying to restore confidence in the broader financial markets. This kind of confidence will come in the form of more normal lending practices and a rebound in economic performance. Some of the darker thinkers believe that a very long, hard road lies ahead. The Organization of Economic Development, which monitors developed country economies, predicts the worst recession since the early 1980s. Economist Joseph Stiglitz, a Nobel Prize winner, forecast that the downturn would be the worst since the Great Depression. Though the road ahead may be harder than most of us are used to, it is unlikely to deviate sharply from previous postwar cyclical downturns. In other words, the economy will eventually recover, as it always has.

FIVE

THE NEW WORLD ORDER

I T'S THE END OF Wall Street—at least the end of the Wall Street that dominated the world of finance from the early 1980s through 2008.

During the past few decades, Wall Street ruled the investment banking world. Whether trading shares for clients or advising on mergers and acquisitions, the Wall Street firms led the way in finance around the globe. Competing banking houses in London, Paris and elsewhere largely disappeared. Barings Bank, the last big British banking firm, collapsed in a trading scandal in February 1995. Outside Wall Street proper, other financial centers, such as London and Hong Kong, grew a great deal, but the dominant players nearly all had a home address in New York. Now the two remaining investment banks, Goldman Sachs and Morgan Stanley, have become bank holding companies and all five former leading firms have shed tens of thousands of jobs.

Indeed, an essential question we're all asking at the dawn of the new world order is how Wall Street's tremendous failure will affect Main Street. As the financial crisis worsened in the fall of 2008, companies and sectors outside finance started to struggle. The credit crunch made it very difficult for even healthy companies to borrow money for their businesses. Weaker companies faced nearly impossible prospects. Circuit City, unable to make it to the Christmas shopping season, filed for bankruptcy protection in November 2008. The carmakers, reeling from declining sales and other financial problems, begged the government for money since they couldn't easily access the credit markets.

Beyond corporate America, local governments began taking action in anticipation of a sharp slowdown. States instituted spending freezes and hiring freezes and talked darkly about looming fiscal deficits. In New York, the heart of the finance industry, the fiscal outlook was particularly grim. No big bonuses on Wall Street meant no big tax haul, and the New York city and state governments had come to count heavily on the big bonus tax payments to make ends meet. Connecticut and New Jersey face similar problems with their bonus-dependent tax receipts.

Though the financial crisis directly affected Wall Street and reshaped that entire industry, the new world order will have an impact on nearly everyone. Jobs are being lost across many sectors, housing prices remain weak, consumer spending is greatly reduced and the overall economic outlook has a grim tone.

Though the changes on Main Street will be very painful for some, the changes on Wall Street will create an entirely different financial landscape. It will take some time to sort out just how the financial system will work. Certainly there will still be advice given for mergers and acquisitions, initial public offerings and the trading of stocks and bonds. But how all that will take place is an open question.

In a spectacular few months, Wall Street blew apart. Bear Stearns scurried meekly into the arms of J.P. Morgan. Lehman Brothers liquidated. Merrill Lynch ran to Bank of America for salvation. Goldman Sachs and Morgan Stanley survived, Morgan Stanley just barely. But even standing amid the wreckage, the final two realized that something had gone awry and registered as bank holding companies with the Federal Reserve System.

Though the worst of the financial crisis—the frightening moments in September and October when Iceland's economy essentially failed and financial markets ceased to function effectively and the worries in October 2008, when it seemed as if liberal democratic capitalism might be over —is behind us, the financial industry will continue to shake itself out over the next several years. Some firms that have weathered the tsunami may yet stumble and fall. Citigroup's prospects, despite massive government assistance, look grim, especially considering the announced layoff of 52,000 employees in November. Many other

GOLDMAN SACHS

Along with Morgan Stanley, Goldman Sachs was the last American investment bank, though it now has registered as a commercial bank and will be regulated under the commercial bank holding acts, thereby officially ending its run as an investment bank.

Started in 1869 as a trading firm in New York, Goldman Sachs followed a circuitous route to become the predominant, most revered firm in the securities industry. After some ups and downs, Goldman was caught in a nasty aspect of the 1929 crash, running a fund that led to widespread losses for many investors when the market crashed. Accused of skullduggery—and worse—Goldman battled to survive the postcrash era and the Great Depression.

Steadily, it rebuilt its reputation, especially in the initial public offering market. It also added research capabilities and enlarged its fixed-income department to include municipal debt. In 1956, Goldman capped its comeback by leading the IPO of the Ford Motor Company.

Through the 1960s, Goldman built out its trading business and expanded underwriting work. The firm nearly lost its footing once again in 1970, when the Penn Central Railroad collapsed. Goldman had issued a lot of debt related to Penn Central, and the ensuing lawsuits nearly bankrupted the firm and its partners.

Despite the Penn Central debacle, Goldman continued to strengthen its position in many areas, notably advisory work in mergers and acquisitions, IPO underwriting, trading and asset management. It also started branching out into other areas, such as private-equity investing, essentially becoming a competitor with many of its advisory and private-equity clients.

As the 1990s unfolded, it became clear that investment banks would have to go public in order to have enough money to compete with larger, commercial banks in the trading, investing and advisory arenas. Goldman was the last major independent investment bank to do so, offering shares to the public in 1999.

During the 2000s, Goldman competed aggressively around the globe to dominate its space. Starting back in the 1970s, it became clear that the main competition would often come from Morgan Stanley. Goldman had always craved Morgan Stanley's impeccable, white-shoe reputation. On the other hand, Morgan Stanley probably craved Goldman's brain factory and its profitability.

In the end, Wall Street veterans would have expressed shock at the demise of the independent investment bank in 2008. But knowing that Goldman and Morgan Stanley were the last two standing would have made sense to anyone.

Goldman's reputation has grown over the past few decades as its star performers have managed to rise high in both political parties. The Democrats boast former Clinton Treasury Secretary Robert Rubin and New Jersey Governor Jon Corzine, among others. The Republicans have Bush Chief of Staff Josh Bolten and Bush Treasury Secretary Henry Paulson, among others.

---

banks continue to carry a great deal of bad real estate–related debt, and many companies need real estate prices to recover sooner than later, a prospect that's admittedly unlikely. Also, even the financial institutions that made it through the crisis now face a global downturn that will cause new difficulties. Mergers, initial public offerings and other core aspects of the financial industry usually fall off sharply during downturns. Trading volumes will also likely remain weak, undercutting potential profit.

As the industry sorts itself out, regulators will go through a similar exercise, trying to sort out its own rules and regulations and come up with a new approach that will help avoid a repeat of the present calamity. Calls for new or smarter regulation abound, and depending on how intense the downturn becomes, regulations are likely to change more profoundly than they have since the 1933 and 1934 acts that still largely govern Wall Street (see sidebar on page 102).

From Wall Street's perspective, and from the financial perspective writ large, one important lesson of the crisis is that it pays to be big—or at least complex. The government showed an exceeding desire to rescue firms "too big" or "too complex" to fail, including Citigroup, AIG and Bear Stearns. Lehman executives must be kicking themselves for not getting bigger or taking even crazier, more complex risks. This, of course, is a mildly cynical view, but in the wake of the financial bailouts and rescues both in the U.S. and abroad, questions about moral hazard are bound to increase.

Regardless of cynicism or moral hazard, the new world of Wall Street will have a handful of behemoths and a number of minnows who establish specialities in key areas such as advising on mergers or helping companies go public. Firms in between will struggle to survive. That means that Goldman Sachs and Morgan Stanley, though proudly independent today, will need to grow by acquiring more businesseses, such as banks, or be gobbled up to remain relevant. Counterintuitively, the two firms might go back to their origins and strip away much of what nearly destroyed them—the trading, the financial wizardry and the exotic investments—and become primarily deal-making advisory firms once more. This is unlikely, given the size of each firm, but the duration and deepness of the economic downturn could make it more likely.

For individuals, huge banks—Bank of America and J.P. Morgan, which owns the Chase retail banking franchise—mean safety. But they generally also mean higher fees and poorer service. For that reason, smaller, nimbler local banks will fight hard to win business from the giants. In the New York area, Commerce Bank used high-touch customer service to grab customers away from banking behemoths such as Chase and Citigroup. Commerce was bought by Toronto-Dominion Bank in the fall of 2007 for $8.5 billion and was renamed TD Bank in November 2008.

J.P. Morgan and Bank of America will face big hurdles integrating their bevy of crisis-related acquisitions, and how they do so will help determine which of the two becomes the top bank in the nation and perhaps the world. Globally, the Japanese banks, with huge assets and apparently few bad debts, could also become big players. Mitsubishi UFJ Financial Group's investment in Morgan Stanley perhaps indicates a willingness among the Japanese banks to become more daring. Of course, being rather plain vanilla helped them avoid much of the recent nastiness.

The many boutique banks, such as Greenhill, Evercore Partners and Lazard, should continue to do fine, as long as they focus on their advisory businesses.

The mutual fund industry is likely to go through a substantial shakeout. With the markets down sharply and investors, especially the tens of millions at or near retirement, badly scorched, interest in mutual funds is expected to diminish. For a long time, a few small firms—Vanguard, Fidelity, Putnam, State Street and others—have dominated the mutual fund industry. The top firms will likely grow larger, with smaller boutiques surviving and many in the great middle withering away amid the widespread retreat from equity investing.

For individuals, the consolidation of mutual funds won't have a big impact. Fees for actively managed mutual funds will remain higher than they should. Fees for index funds, such as those pioneered by Vanguard, will remain reasonably low. Most people will continue to tap into mutual funds primarily through their 401(k)s, and a winnowing of the massive fund industry shouldn't have a large impact on 401(k)s since that business is dominated by just a handful of firms, such as Fidelity, Vanguard and State Street.

There's no question that regulation will change. Things have thus far moved too quickly and too sharply for regulators to stop, breathe and figure out what to do differently. But with Democrats holding the White House and Congress, regulatory reform seems very likely.

Creating new regulations that will eliminate greed is practically impossible, but that doesn't mean politicians won't try. In the 1990s, Congress set up new rules that taxed executive salaries over $1 million at a high rate in a bid to fight greed. Companies simply set up generous stock option packages and various retirement goodies to get around the new rules. Regulations, however, can create a level playing field that promotes fair competition. Clearly, whatever we had in place failed mightily to address the financial crisis or prevent it from occurring. Expect a review of all financial regulations, going back to bedrock principles. The basic starting point will be: What we have didn't work and helped contribute to the near collapse in our system. What should we do differently?

An interesting aspect of financial markets, especially in the past eight years, is how aggressively money moved into the unregulated sphere. Much of the financial industry's regulatory framework focuses on financial markets. But most of the trading and investing at the heart of the financial crisis took place away from the financial markets, in the so-called over-the-counter markets. "Over the counter" simply means unregulated trading that takes place off market, usually between a bank and an institutional investor. Almost all the complex derivative products that intersected with the financial crisis trade in this kind of market. Those unwatched markets boomed while the more heavily regulated stock and bond markets grew more slowly. After new post-Enron regulation, many commentators argued that the U.K. was winning financial market business at the expense of the more heavily regulated U.S. financial markets.

Indeed, in 2006, just before the storm hit, most of Wall Street feared that the U.S. regulatory environment would eventually erode New York's ability to compete globally. Those overseas felt much the same way, with the U.K. boasting of its "soft-touch" regulatory approach and Hong Kong noting how it could handle large Chinese companies' initial public offerings without New York's help.

This, of course, all changed in the wake of the financial crisis. What that means is that all the developed markets will now reexamine their regulatory policies. Those that can do it well and intelligently will stand to attract more business than those that take a more ham-fisted approach.

Some have called for a restoration of Glass-Steagall, the regulation that prohibited commercial banks to own and operate investment banks. This seems impractical in an age of highly integrated financial markets. Moreover, if Glass-Steagall had not been eliminated, many of the rescues of the past year, notably those of Merrill Lynch and Bear Stearns, would not have been possible, because only large banks had the resources to acquire those securities firms. If Merrill Lynch, Lehman Brothers and Bear Stearns had all gone under without rescue, the chance of outright financial system collapse would have been greatly magnified.

A QUICK HISTORY OF REGULATION

When financial panics occur, the common response is a call for more regulation. And most of the regulation that governs the finance world can be tied to specific calamities, controversies and corruption.

Curiously enough, there was scant regulation in the finance

sector until the 20th century. During the stock market crisis of 1907, J. P. Morgan himself emerged to save the day by pooling investors to stem the fear-based selling that had besieged the market. Given that even J. P. Morgan was not immortal, the government moved to establish the Federal Reserve System in 1913 to oversee the banking sector by setting various business rules, funding requirements and lending guidelines, though the stock market remained mostly unwatched.

In the wake of the 1929 stock market crash, which impoverished many people, including newly minted individual investors, the government passed laws that formed the core of the investment regulatory scheme. The Securities Acts of 1933 and 1934 established the Securities and Exchange Commission to oversee the investment arena. They also required that companies provide more information to potential investors, especially before going public.

The 1933 and 1934 acts have changed over the decades, but the basic framework remains today.

Following the collapse of Enron, Congress augmented securities rules by passing the Sarbanes-Oxley Act. This new set of rules established stiffer oversight for the accounting industry and tougher reporting requirements for public companies. In addition, state regulators became more active during this time. Former New York Attorney General Eliot Spitzer launched several probes aimed at Wall Street during his tenure, leading to rule changes governing investment research, mutual fund trading and the sale of insurance.

In the wake of the financial crisis, regulatory reform will certainly be on the agenda once again. Already, all the remaining investment banks have converted themselves to bank holding companies, placing them under the regulatory purview of the Federal Reserve. More changes are likely as policy makers sort through the mess.

In the U.S., it would be ideal to update the regulations to match the sophistication of the marketplace, especially the emphasis on debt-related instruments. Certainly this trading has slowed, but it will return in some form. Traditionally, regulatory reform has simply meant more regulations and regulators. It would be shrewd to start over and discuss what exactly is the right kind of regulation and remake the system in the cleanest, most technologically sophisticated way possible. Grafting onto the old system, which is creaking under its seventy-five years of legacy, would simply create a regulatory behemoth without actually addressing the issues of the 21st century in an intelligent manner.

Two other aspects of regulation can expect examination. First, insurance is currently overseen state by state. In the wake of the calamity at the insurer AIG and other large insurance companies, such as Fortis, expect Washington to look at nationalizing this oversight. Insurance companies, by and large, have fared better than banks, which already have national oversight, but logic doesn't always dictate action in Washington.

Second, hedge funds could come in for more scrutiny. More lightly regulated than mutual funds, hedge funds sometimes become the target of companies angry at their tactics. Specifically, hedge funds that go short, or bet on share price declines, received widespread blame for rumormongering and other tactics that drove companies like Lehman Brothers to disaster. In response to the crisis in September 2008, the government banned short selling in a number of financial companies and soon after widened that ban to include other companies. The ban on short selling was lifted in October 2008.

This ban, however, created a number of problems. Primarily, it reduced the liquidity of some stocks and eventually led regulators to end the ban earlier than expected.

Still, hedge funds, and short-selling hedge funds in particular, remain a popular target of market critics. Even though hedge funds seemed to suffer less than heavily regulated mutual funds, they can expect scrutiny from a Democratic administration.

Main Street

Main Street has watched Wall Street's woes in a manner different from other crises. This time, more Main Streeters than ever had a slice of the action. Through 401(k)s and other retirement investment vehicles, more individuals than ever own shares. Seeing so much wealth disappear so fast has radically changed their mood.

People are spending less. Retail sales have plunged, car sales have skidded and everyone is scrimping here and saving there in anticipation that the downturn will prove long-lasting. Individuals will grapple with how best to save for retirement and how to protect their home. (See Chapter 8, "On Investment Strategy.")

As the government extends its bailouts to include credit card companies, automakers and others not seemingly involved in the meat of the financial crisis, lots of folks on Main Street want to know when *their* rescue is coming.

At the same time, those who have been living prudently and

aren't facing severe problems are angered that reckless neighbors will be bailed out by taxpayer dollars coming largely from the prudent class.

How all these angers and resentments play out in the coming months and years will hinge a great deal on what happens in the financial markets. If the markets' health returns and retirement accounts become more robust, much will be forgiven. If, however, stock prices remain low and begin to behave as they did from 1929 to 1954—the period it took for stock prices to regain their pre–1929 crash highs—expect much agitating and calls for change. There is a lot of resentment simmering out there, both among those needing help and those who find themselves doing the helping.

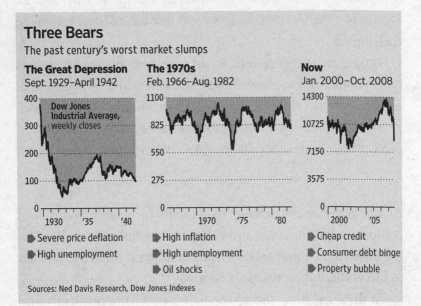

Three Bears
The past century's worst market slumps

The Great Depression
Sept. 1929–April 1942

The 1970s
Feb. 1966–Aug. 1982

Now
Jan. 2000–Oct. 2008

Dow Jones Industrial Average, weekly closes

- Severe price deflation
- High unemployment

- High inflation
- High unemployment
- Oil shocks

- Cheap credit
- Consumer debt binge
- Property bubble

Sources: Ned Davis Research, Dow Jones Indexes

FAQ

Wall Street dominated global finance. Who will dominate it now?

Wall Street firms will still play a role; there just aren't as many of them anymore. Goldman Sachs, and perhaps Morgan Stanley, will compete for business with huge entities such as Bank of America–Merrill Lynch–Countrywide, J.P. Morgan Chase–Bear Stearns–Washington Mutual and Wells Fargo–Wachovia. Citigroup remains huge, even though it hasn't gobbled up much of significance during the turmoil. Goldman and Morgan will also face overseas players such as Deutsche Bank, HSBC and Barclays, which acquired much of Lehman Brothers. In the end, the playing field will contain fewer players and have more of a global flavor than ever before.

Will any more banks or investment banks fail?

Yes. Smaller banks, certainly, face the prospect of failure. And larger banks, despite help from the government in terms of capital injections, are not entirely out of the woods—and one of the really big banks could still very well fail. As for investment banks, now that Goldman and Morgan Stanley are officially bank holding companies, what is left is only minnowlike boutique firms. Some of them could fail, but this would hardly cause a ripple.

FAQ

Will anybody from the failed companies at the heart of the financial crisis go to jail?

Unlike Enron, in which corruption took place, it presently appears that the financial crisis stemmed from the common elements of past panics: overconfidence and greed. Neither overconfidence nor greed, at least currently, is against the law. That doesn't mean the feds won't look extremely hard for bad actors. Already the SEC, the FBI and other state and national regulators are probing Lehman Brothers, AIG, hedge funds and other elements of the financial system. Historically, financial crises, such as the one we are going through now lead to some sort of criminal action against individuals, companies or both. On Wall Street, they call this "making a sacrifice to the market gods." It remains unclear what that sacrifice will be.

When will the regulations change?

It's going to take some time. Recall that after the 1929 crash, it took until 1933 to pass the first securities act. Things move both faster and more slowly today. And given the global nature of the crisis, politicians will want to balance bloodlust against long-term competitive realities. If a timetable similar to that of 1929 is followed, we

FAQ

could see a bevy of new regulations in 2011 and 2012, just as the next presidential campaign is getting under way.

Does the recent crisis mean that capitalism is doomed?
The center nearly didn't hold, and this is as close as the system has come to failure since the 1930s. The system has problems, and even devotees, such as past Federal Reserve chief Alan Greenspan, have expressed alarm at how the system broke down. The difficulty is that other systems, notably socialism and communism, haven't demonstrated superior benefits. China and Russia have adopted a modified capitalistic approach, called authoritarian or autocratic capitalism. In the recent tsunami, that did little to help Russia as its stock market crashed and trading was halted for days. China seemed to weather the storm a bit better than most, but its lack of transparency makes it difficult to judge just how well China is doing.

Why so many references to the 1930s? Are we looking at another Great Depression?
The severe problems in the financial markets, their global nature and their scope of damage force everyone to look back to the 1930s. Every panic or recession since then has seemed too small or too contained to present an apt com-

FAQ

parison. It is unsettling to read so many references to that era of migrating Okies and long soup lines. At this point, most economists expect a sharp, deep recession, with growth starting to come back later in 2009. Economists are often wrong—one Wall Street aphorism has economists predicting five out of the next three recessions—but it's hard to envision a scenario of 25% unemployment, which is what occurred in the Great Depression.

What does the new world look like from Main Street?
Government tax receipts at the federal and state levels are likely to diminish, which will place pressure on various government services from health care to education to law enforcement. That stress on government services will come as the bad economy forces more and more individuals to rely on those services to get by. More individuals will find their deposits taken over by other banks as failures and consolidation change that business. And more individuals will take a cautious, less risky approach to spending, investing and saving.

SIX

WHAT IS SAFE?

NOT ONLY HAS THE financial crisis changed the landscape of Wall Street, it's changed the way everyone thinks about money. Although understanding what happened and its impact is a necessary starting place, the next step is getting one's own house in financial order. Though no one asked for the crisis to occur, it does present an opportunity to learn—and in some cases relearn—important lessons about personal finance. Contrary to what a lot of us had come to believe, the stock market is neither a bank nor a safe; holding on to too much expensive debt, whether in our homes or in our portfolios, is unwise; and it always makes sense to put a little away for a rainy day.

Of course, getting some perspective on the situation is a good start. People are understandably angry and a bit frightened by what's taken place. A lot of retirees are being forced into going back to work, many who want to retire can't and everyone's wondering just what are safe investments and what are not as financial companies collapse around us. For instance, if the insurance giant AIG should fail, how safe is your life insurance policy? The good news, detailed more below, is that it's actually a lot safer than you probably think.

In an effort to combat the financial crisis, the government has made all sorts of moves to expand both explicit and implicit guarantees for companies and individuals, to try to make people feel safer about their money. The biggest move was its takeover of Fannie Mae and Freddie Mac. By taking over these two huge issuers of mortgages, the government added more than $5 trillion in mortgages to its balance sheet. This part of the rescue is aimed at reducing mortgage rates by eliminating the possibility that either Fannie Mae or Freddie Mac might fail.

As you rethink your personal finances in this crazy climate, assessing the safety of your assets and investments is fundamental. So let's start by taking a look at what's safe and what's not. After that, we'll look at strategies for tackling debt, and finally we will talk about investment strategies for our new age.

Remarkably, the question "What is safe?" hasn't had a long airing since the Great Depression. Back in those dark days, thousands of banks failed and millions of people saw their life savings evaporate. Do we stand such a risk today? No. There are now many programs in place to protect individuals, the best known being insurance on cash deposits in banks. But there are also various protections for your investments, insurance and other accounts.

Savings and Checking Accounts and CDs

The government, through the Federal Deposit Insurance Corporation, insures cash deposits in many accounts, including checking, savings, and certificates of deposit. Prior to the financial crisis, individual accounts were insured up to $100,000. As part of its confidence-building measures, that maximum was temporarily raised to $250,000 per account. (You may have received such a notification from your bank if you've recently made a transaction.) There's a good chance that "temporary" will evolve into permanent.

The last previous change came in the wake of the savings-and-loan collapse of the late 1980s and early 1990s, when the insurance increased from $40,000 to $100,000.

The insurance, however, doesn't apply if you accumulate more than the maximum in one account and the bank fails. When California's IndyMac bank failed in the summer of 2008, some account holders ended up losing money because their accounts were over the insurance cap. This is less likely today with the higher cap but still possible if individuals don't monitor their accounts to keep them under the cap. This, of course, is a high-class problem that doesn't affect very many Americans. If only more of us had to worry about our huge cash savings, but alas many of us have a lot of debt. According to the Federal Reserve, the average American household carries about $8,000 in usually very expensive credit-card debt.

The FDIC insurance system, however, does not guarantee that your bank won't fail—it simply guarantees that you won't lose your money should this come to pass. People with accounts at the failed IndyMac learned this reality firsthand, and the strength of the FDIC program means the U.S. hasn't seen the same kinds of bank runs that have taken place in other countries such as Great Britain and Iceland.

THE FDIC

A longtime investor remarked in 2008, "I never thought it would reach the point where we worried about cash deposits in major banks." But the financial crisis did get that bad. In some parts of the developed world, questions about cash deposits in major banks lingered into 2009.

The Great Depression taught many lessons, one of the biggest being that bank runs can feed on themselves, quickly creating a very difficult to control phenomenon that can lay waste to companies, the economy and people. In 1933, with bank runs common, about 4,000 banks and 1,700 Savings & Loans failed, according to the FDIC. Families, small businesses and others lost everything.

Today, such an outcome is very unlikely, at least in the U.S. Amid the banking crisis of 1933, new regulations created the Federal Deposit Insurance Corp. The FDIC's job was to guarantee bank deposits, making bank runs less likely. The idea is that if bank deposits are guaranteed, there is no need to run to your own bank just because others are failing.

Banks are vulnerable to runs because they do not keep all their deposit assets in their vaults. If they did, they'd just be one big concrete mattress, and a pretty expensive one at that. In order to make money, banks must invest or lend out their assets to others. That means that if everyone arrives at once to remove their deposits, their deposits wouldn't be readily available, even though a well-run bank could recover the assets and make them available in fairly short order, by borrowing from either other banks or the Federal Reserve system.

The FDIC's guarantees have risen over time, and in the wake of the recent financial crisis, the guaranteed amount per account has risen from $100,000 to $250,000. It's important to note that the FDIC guarantees only cash—not stocks or bonds.

Having a bank insurance program doesn't mean banks can't fail. Indeed, some blame the insurance of accounts on the savings-and-loan debacle of the late 1980s and early 1990s. This was the first test of the insurance system since it was established in the early 1930s.

Some S&L operators, counting on the deposit guarantees and lax oversight, grew increasingly reckless with their investment strategies. Ultimately, a great many S&Ls failed, and the S&L deposit insurance program, a sister organization to the FDIC, went defunct and was absorbed into the FDIC.

The FDIC funds itself by charging banks a fee, based on the amount of deposits a bank has. That fund, however, has been severely depleted during the current financial crisis. When the Federal Reserve swiftly approved Wells Fargo's acquisition of Wachovia, the fund didn't have enough money to cover a Wachovia failure. J.P. Morgan Chase's absorption of Washington Mutual (WaMu) avoided a similar problem earlier in the year.

Not surprisingly, the FDIC has pushed hard for mortgage relief programs aimed at individuals. These mortgages are at the heart of problems within the banking industry, which remains fragile despite improvements in late 2008. Most experts believe the FDIC will soon need a large infusion of cash, most likely from a combination of taxpayer money and industry fees, to maintain its credibility.

Given the scope of the banking crisis, however, the FDIC may find it needs more money to remain solvent. It charges banks a small premium to build its asset base and uses that money to insure savings accounts at failed banks. After a number of rescues large and small, the FDIC funds shrank to a precarious position. Regulators have avoided tapping out the FDIC by forcing failing banks such as Washington Mutual into the arms of healthier suitors. In WaMu's case, J.P. Morgan Chase bought the bank. Similarly, Wells Fargo acquired the teetering Wachovia. The outright failure of WaMu or Wachovia would have put a severe strain on the FDIC. Should the FDIC run into funding problems, the most likely solution is a combination of a government infusion of cash and an increase in the premiums paid by healthy banks. In other words, almost nobody expects that the FDIC insurance program would itself have failed, so you shouldn't worry about the assets in your savings, checking or CD accounts.

You can learn more about the FDIC at www.fdic.gov.

Money Market Accounts

Government insurance used to stop at the accounts mentioned above. Though regulations guarded against corruption and other bad practices, marketplace risk took center stage in other accounts. For instance, U.S. Treasury bonds are not guaranteed by any insurance, but they are considered extremely safe because the U.S. has never defaulted on its debt and few people expect it will do so in the future. After all, the government can simply print more money to pay its debt. This isn't the best economic approach, of course, but it is a last resort the government can always employ.

For decades, money market funds were also considered extremely safe. These funds invested in highly rated short-term debt, such as commercial paper. Many individuals employ money market accounts in a manner similar to their checking or savings account, as a holder of ready cash. From time to time, these funds have run into some problems, but their safety rating has always remained high. Money market funds are priced at $1 per share, and holding that line has always been considered sacrosanct—that is, it was until Lehman Brothers collapsed and some huge money market funds that got caught with too much Lehman Brothers debt that no longer had any value "broke the buck." The failure of these money market funds, the biggest being Reserve Primary money market fund with $64.8 billion in assets, spooked investors and prompted the government to offer insurance on funds that wanted to participate in an insurance program.

This extension of government insurance, another example of the government reaching deep into its pockets to reassure the marketplace, may or may not be temporary. And most, but not all, money market funds are participating in the insurance program. You need to check with your fund or your broker to find out the status of your particular fund.

One chief motive for the government intervention in the money markets was to improve the overall credit environment. In the wake of the money market fund failures, healthier money market funds refrained from purchasing short-term debt, fearing that they would be exposed to too much risk. Short-term debt, such as commercial paper, is a little like oil in the economic engine. Businesses use this debt to fund operations, make payroll payments and manage resources. Without this market, the cost of doing business can rise sharply, forcing companies to find savings elsewhere, meaning layoffs, business closures and other difficult maneuvers. At the height of the commercial paper crunch, even healthy firms such as General Electric found it difficult to do business. That meant borrowing money became much more expensive for those firms, curtailing their ability to expand their businesses or hire new staff. Similar problems occurred at AT&T and elsewhere. The government's offer to guarantee money market funds helped loosen this market, which alleviated one aspect of the credit crunch.

Brokerage Accounts

Many investors are surprised to discover that their investment holdings have no guarantee and no insurance. There are regulations that guard against corruption and other malfeasance, but individuals face market risk in these accounts. As we saw in 2008, that market risk can be quite painful.

But what happens if your brokerage firm fails, as Lehman Brothers did in 2008? Your accounts are protected by the Securities Investor Protection Corp. (SIPC). SIPC is funded by member firms and guarantees that individual identifiable security holdings are not lost when a firm collapses. Usually SIPC works with the Securities and Exchange Commission, the nation's top securities regulator, to ensure the smooth transfer of accounts. You should make sure that your broker is a member of SIPC because some smaller outfits are not.

SIPC also has a reserve fund to address other outstanding claims in the event of a brokerage firm failure. The cap on an individual claim is $500,000, with a $100,000 maximum for cash claims. SIPC was established in 1970, and through the end of 2006, it said it advanced $505 million in order to make possible the recovery of $15.7 billion in assets for an estimated 626,000 investors. The Lehman Brothers failure will no doubt increase those figures substantially.

More details about SIPC are available at www.sipc.org, and more information about investor protections can also be found at the Securities and Exchange Commission Web site, www.sec .gov, and the National Association of Securities Dealers Web site, www.nasd.com.

Mutual Funds

Mutual funds held in a brokerage account fall under the same protections that the SIPC provides for those accounts. Also, mutual fund assets are held "in custody" for investors, meaning that if a mutual fund company itself collapses, your assets would not become part of any bankruptcy proceedings; they would still be your assets.

Contrary to what some investors believe, however, mutual funds are not guaranteed to succeed. If stock prices decline, odds are that your mutual funds will also suffer. This is part of the risk investors take on when they invest in the stock market. Mutual funds can add diversification to your portfolio, thereby theoretically limiting your risk. But they do not eliminate the market risk inherent in investing.

The one exception to this is money market mutual funds, which, as explained above, can opt to participate in a government insurance program that offers some guarantees.

Retirement Accounts

Most people own mutual funds in their 401(k), 403(b) or IRA plans. The same rules that protect your assets should a fund administrator or IRA manager collapse apply to these holdings. In addition, should your own company fail, you are protected by the same rules.

Of course, there are a few risks to bear in mind with your retirement account. Many individuals invest in their own companies through their retirement accounts. Since the company is already giving you a paycheck, this is usually an increase of investment risk not worth taking. When Enron went bust, a number of employees suffered badly because they'd invested heavily in Enron through their 401(k)s.

Also, there's some risk that a corporate matching payment to your 401(k) plan could get snaggled into a bankruptcy proceeding should your company fail. This would happen if the matching payment was "in process" when the company failed. In that case, you'd need to get into the creditors' line to recover it. Employees generally have better standing than most creditors in a bankruptcy workout, but those workouts take time.

Some companies have also moved to eliminate their matching funds to save money. This obviously hurts employees, but it may help a company stay alive through tough times, which is probably more important in the near term than the company match.

Last, there's investment risk in your retirement account if

you hold investment securities, such as mutual funds. If the market goes down, your funds generally aren't immune to that.

Insurance

Insurance comes in many forms, and you'd think from its name that it's pretty safe. And generally it is. There are many forms of insurance, but basically insurance requires the payment of a small monthly premium with a payout in the event of death or some other insurance-related event, such as a home fire in the case of home insurance holders.

What happens if your insurance company goes bust? The situation is rare, but in late 2008 the property and casualty insurance giant AIG ran aground, requiring more than $100 billion in government loans to remain afloat. Millions of individuals and companies have AIG insurance accounts, so its outright collapse would affect a huge swathe of people.

Insurance is backed on a state-by-state basis by the National Conference of Insurance Guaranty Funds. These state funds, created about 40 years ago, do have limits, similar to the limits on cash deposit accounts, generally about $100,000 per policy, rising to $300,000 for death benefits. These caps are state by state, so it's smart to check your state insurance commissioner's Web site for details. According to its Web site, the Guaranty Funds system has paid out about $21 billion in about six hundred property and casualty insolvencies since 1976. Similar to deposit insurance, the Guaranty Funds are funded by life insurance companies.

Each state also has a regulator who oversees the insurance industry, and they work together through the National Association of Insurance Commissioners. The Kansas Insurance Department Web site provides an answer to a common question about policyholder protections:

> State regulators have a variety of tools available if it appears an insurer is not going to be able to fulfill its promises to policyholders. Your state regulator can take over management of an insurer through conservation or rehabilitation. Even if liquidation of an insurance company is necessary, policyholder claims will generally be paid either by the insurance company or by a guaranty fund, which all states have in place to provide coverage to policyholders.

This and answers to other common questions can be found at http://www.ksinsurance.org/gpa/news/2008/AIG_9–18.pdf. More information is available at the National Association of Insurance Commissioners at www.naic.org. Also, you can check out details of the insurance for policyholders at the National Conference of Insurance Guaranty Funds at www.ncigf.org.

Annuities

Annuities are investment vehicles that require an investment up front and guarantee a certain rate of return in the future. For instance, you can put $100,000 into an annuity, and it will pay you out a fixed percentage of that amount over the life of the annuity. This is a popular investment among retirees and some younger people, but critics frequently harp on the high fee structures annuities sport when compared with mutual funds. Of course, in the wake of the financial crisis and the crushing of the stock market, fees may matter a lot less to some folks than actually getting a return.

The regulations and guaranty funds that protect insurance policyholders also apply to annuities, primarily because annuities are sold by insurance companies. A snag with annuities, as opposed to cash deposits and regular investments, is that they are expensive to exit if you become worried about the health of your insurer. There are early-withdrawal fees, tax consequences and other costs associated with early withdrawal from an annuity.

Commodities, Futures and Options

Commodities, futures and options are more exotic investments than simple stocks, bonds or mutual funds. Gold and oil are commodities, and they most commonly trade in the futures markets. For instance, when you hear oil priced on the news, it is almost always the price for a future delivery of oil on a specific date, not the cash price that day. Options are similar to futures, giving the investor a chance to buy or sell a stock or bond or some other financial instrument in the future. The chief difference between futures and options is that an owner of a futures contract *must* take delivery of what the futures contract represents—oil, corn or gold, for instance—whereas an option holder has the *right but not the obligation* to acquire whatever the option represents, oftentimes the option to purchase a stock at a set price on a certain date.

Most investors hold commodity investments in their brokerage accounts through investment funds or commodities futures. The protections offered by SIPC apply to those accounts if the brokerage firm is liquidated. Options and futures exchanges, where commodities and other derivatives are traded, also require that customer accounts be cordoned off to protect investors in the case of a firm failure.

The Commodity Futures Trading Commission is the main regulatory body overseeing the commodities and futures markets; see www.cftc.gov.

Hedge Funds

Though the rules against fraud apply, there are limited protections for investors in hedge funds should these funds collapse. This is one reason that regulations limit individual investors' participation in hedge funds. When a hedge fund goes kerblooey, claims are usually settled through litigation, which can be lengthy and expensive.

Some individuals have indirect exposure to hedge funds through a pension program. Ideally, your pension fund should be diversified enough to sustain any outright hedge fund failures.

Your Home

You can insure your home against a calamity such as a fire, but it is very difficult to protect the value of your home. There are some real estate futures instruments that trade on the Chicago Mercantile Exchange, but these are designed primarily for large players in the real estate market, such as real estate investment trusts and property developers. As long as you have bought a home you can afford, the old-fashioned notion of shelter is the best and most prudent thing a home has to offer.

FAQ

Are my cash deposits safe?

Cash deposits are insured up to $250,000 per individual, which means the vast majority of deposits are safe. Even if your bank fails, your deposits will be transferred to a healthier institution and you will have access to them.

What protections are there if my brokerage firm goes bust?

The SIPC protects investors' accounts and makes sure that they are moved to a healthier institution, where investors can access them. Though your investments are not safe from market fluctuations, SIPC, the SEC and other financial system regulators have a strong track record of protecting individual accounts, even through the recent financial crisis.

Is my insurance policy still good if the insurance company fails?

For the most part, yes. Insurance is regulated state by state, and each state has a guaranty program and an insurance commissioner who works to protect policyholders in the case of an insurance company failure. The guaranty system has a strong track record of protecting policies in a manner similar to that of the FDIC. Each state has its own

FAQ

rules, and you should check the state insurance commissioner Web site to know the limits of your protection.

What government programs might help me with my mortgage payments?

Such programs are still being debated and the government has announced plans to buy mortgages in order to drive mortgage rates down. The government has also encouraged many banks to defer foreclosures or some payments. But you can also reach out to your bank to renegotiate the terms of your mortgage. This has gotten trickier since many mortgages are now frequently resold and repackaged. Still, Citigroup, J.P. Morgan Chase and other big lenders have signaled a desire to work with homeowners to reduce the possibility of default, and many homeowners have reworked their payment programs.

Will the government run out of money funding all these bailout and insurance programs?

There's almost no chance that this will happen. The government has tremendous power to raise money (through taxes) and create money (by printing more of it). It is likely to use these tools in order to ensure that its programs stay solvent.

CHECKLIST TO DETERMINE
THE SAFETY OF YOUR ASSETS

1. Make sure your cash deposit accounts are below the $250,000 per account insurance level.

2. Check with your state insurance commissioner Web site to ensure that your policies fall within the state guarantees in case your insurance company fails.

3. Make sure your investment accounts are held at a safe institution. Although SIPC does offer protections, it is best to have your portfolio housed at a healthy institution.

4. Make sure you have paper records of all your assets and a record of where they are held. You need to take responsibility for your own affairs, especially during a time of crisis such as we're seeing. Don't depend on anyone else to look after this for you.

5. Some people leave their 401(k) program behind at a company they previously worked for. This is considered safe, but it's important to keep careful records of such accounts. For extra safety, rolling your retirement programs into a single location may make more sense. Talk with your 401(k) program administrator about your options.

SEVEN

DEBT AND DESTRUCTION

F OR ALL ITS COMPLEXITY, the financial crisis was triggered by one thing: an overabundance of easy money. For companies, that meant a borrowing binge that is coming home to roost in ugly ways, especially in the financial industry. For individuals, that means most of us have carried far too much debt and probably still have too much of it.

The decline in the housing market has compounded the debt problems. Many folks not only have credit card bills stacked on their dining room table, they also have mortgages higher than the current value of their home. This phenomenon of "being underwater" has had a serious impact on consumer confidence. And that has led to changes in consumer behavior. Credit is no longer cool, and thrift is back in.

Thrift, of course, is a good notion—and one that's certainly overdue. Americans have for some time spent more than they've made, leading to the first so-called negative savings rates since the 1930s. This overspending, driven largely by borrowed money, occurred in the corporate and financial sectors as well. As individuals rediscover thrift, companies are going through their own process of "deleveraging" or reducing their credit-bingeing ways.

All this reining in of spending and borrowing has an impact on the broader economic picture, especially as it relates to consumers. Consumer spending makes up 70% of the nation's economic activity, according to government figures. We buy the things that many people make both here and overseas. A thrifty American consumer is certainly not what China, Japan or other great exporting nations want to see.

In some ways, thrift is paradoxical. If everyone is too thrifty, the economy can grind itself into a nasty slowdown. Obviously, a nation that borrows and spends like drunken sailors isn't exactly healthy, either. The recipe for a robust economy is a mixture of old-fashioned thrift and prudent consumption with a sprinkling of splurging here and there. After all, even a thrifty person wants to get her nails done once in a while.

The rise of thrift is stemming from a sense that people are less rich than before, even if there has been no real change in their employment status, homes or income. Certainly there's been a reduction in investment portfolios and retirement plans, and this would explain why a person's financial psychology changes even when day-to-day circumstances don't change. A reduction of spending, of course, is sometimes driven by more than just mind games. A tougher credit environment has contributed to a dramatic drop in car purchases. Soaring gasoline prices led Americans to drive less for the first time in decades, though gasoline prices dropped dramatically in the last half of 2008, giving the consumer at least one break.

In midyear 2008, some commentators argued that the psychology attached to falling home values and investment portfolios wouldn't have a big impact. Stronger-than-expected second-quarter growth and retail sales seemed to buttress that case. But as I write this in December 2008, consumer spending has declined markedly in the last several months and prospects for the Christmas shopping season are bleak. But, interestingly, shoppers flooded stores after Thanksgiving and aggressive discounting has had more people purchasing presents than dour economists had initially forecast.

Still, the current financial crisis is widely called the worst since the Great Depression. As the psychology of difficult times sinks in deeper, more people will find small ways to save a buck here or there. Lenders will remain stingy and may become even more so. All of this can dangerously feed on itself if fears rise. When Franklin D. Roosevelt declared, "The only thing we have to fear is fear itself" upon taking office in 1932, he was talking directly to people's psychology about money. If everyone put their money in a mattress and banks feared to lend, growth would not return. Mr. Roosevelt's plea, however, did not work as he hoped. The economy remained mired in dire straits for another eight years despite fireside chats, massive works programs and large infusions of government spending. Fear, once it takes hold, can be difficult to reverse.

It's hard to envision things getting to that level today, but there's little question that fear about the future is having a negative impact on consumer and corporate psychology.

But the most important thing to do in the months ahead is focus less on the national scene and more on your own situation. Weathering this storm means keeping your assets safe and reducing your debt so you have a stronger personal finance situation. Also, it is when others are panicking that the calm thrive. Those who have prudently prepared for a rainy day are in a position today to acquire deeply discounted homes and cheap stocks.

Let's take a run through all the types of debt that you face and discuss strategies for paring back your debt. Reducing your debt should be your number one personal finance goal. Once you have your debt under control, it makes sense to look at your savings and figure out how best to invest them. There are, of course, exceptions to the reduce-debt-first rule, primarily as it relates to retirement accounts and how they function. For instance, if your company offers a matching grant to your 401(k) contributions, it makes sense to take advantage of that free money at the expense of some debt reduction. Free money doesn't come along very often, as we've all learned, so it's best to grab it when it is available.

Credit Cards

Credit cards are the most pernicious of debt vehicles. At first they seem like a wonder, but too many people find themselves lugging big balances and paying large interest payments for years after they innocently sign up for a card with its promises of 0% interest rate, air miles, and bonuses galore. Sometimes the mismanagement of credit card debt can drive people into personal bankruptcy. Even short of that, maintaining large balances and paying high interest rates eats into other, more important uses for your money, namely saving and planning for your retirement.

But there are some basic strategies you can employ to start reducing your credit card debt. For starters, pretend that gasoline is still $4 a gallon, and use the savings at the pump to pay down debts. If gasoline is $2 a gallon where you live now, set aside $2 for each gallon purchased—that's what you were spending in the beginning of 2007—and use that money to pay off debts.

Second, look at the interest rates you are paying and compare them with the interest rates you are receiving in any cash deposit accounts, such as a savings or checking account. The odds are that you are paying much more credit card interest than you are getting from the bank. Though savings are important, there's a false sense of security when you carry savings *and* large credit card debt at the same time. After all, if you aggressively pay down your credit card debt and suddenly face a financial emergency, you can always re-up the credit card debt.

Meantime, you will have saved money on the interest rate differential between your bank account and your credit card debt.

Second, many credit cards offer a free transfer and lower introductory rates after you transfer your debt to the new home. The credit card companies are banking on your maintaining a high level of debt and not bolting when the introductory rate rises. Also, many introductory rates disappear if you are late or miss a payment. While you are paying down your credit cards, you can use the free transfer strategy to take advantage of various lower-rate offers. It is important, however, to be diligent about your monthly payments, otherwise this strategy will backfire.

A third strategy is to borrow money at a cheaper rate to pay off your expensive credit card debt. This has gotten tougher in the credit crunch since lenders have become far stingier. Also, with home prices falling, the ability to take money out of your home at a lower rate to pay high-rate credit card debt is more doubtful. Still, not all lending has ended, so it's worth exploring this possibility with your local bank.

A last strategy is credit card debt consolidation. Many people have several credit cards, and there's a temptation to consolidate these cards into a single payment. Many credit card debt consolidators have become expert at appearing soothing and helpful in their pitch to consumers. Their main pitch: that the monthly payments in a credit card debt consolidation are smaller than the total monthly payments on your cards. But you pay a steep price in two ways: the interest rate doesn't change much, if at all, and the consolidation simply extends your payments so that you end up paying far more in interest than you would have without consolidating. Sometimes this is the only option for people in tough straits. This technique should be viewed as a last resort, but if it's your only option, it's a step in the right direction.

Mortgages and Other House-Related Debt

Most homeowners financed their purchases with a mortgage. For a long time, mortgages had few exotic features. Purchasers had to "put down" 20% of the home's sale price, and then the bank would finance the remainder of the purchase with a long-term mortgage, the standard length being 30 years. The structure of the traditional mortgage has several benefits. By putting 20% down, the owner acquires an immediate equity stake in the home. If the value of the home declines, odds are that the down payment will mean you still have some equity in the home. The 30-year term helps stretch payments out, enabling investors to more easily become homeowners.

These positive notions became radically twisted during the housing bubble. Though many people took the traditional route, a great many did not. People with lousy credit—or no credit—took out subprime mortgages. Banks offered mortgages with no down payment, skippable payments and interest-only payments, and many of these mortgages went bad when people couldn't afford them.

On top of these mortgages, a lot of people also took out home-equity loans and/or home-equity lines of credit. When home values were high or rising, these worked beautifully. As home values dropped, these versions of debt became weighty anchors.

All around the country, foreclosure rates have skyrocketed. A lot of homeowners, owing more on their homes than they are worth, have simply walked away from their mortgages. Others are scrambling to hold on to their homes in tough circumstances.

Traditionally, home values weaken when the unemployment picture worsens. This time, home values declined ahead of rising unemployment. With job losses mounting, the home market could face more tough times ahead.

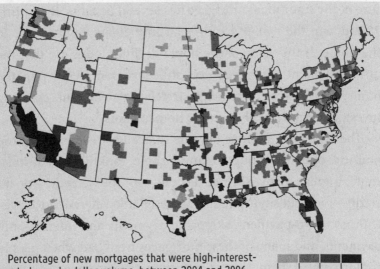

Percentage of new mortgages that were high-interest-rate loans, by dollar volume, between 2004 and 2006, when the U.S. housing market was peaking.

5% 15% 20% 25% 40%

Note: Areas shown are metropolitan statistical areas

Source: Home Mortgage Disclosure Act data

Debt Trouble

Selected metropolitan areas with high proportions of new high-rate mortgages, 2004-2006

Metropolitan Statistical Area	Number of high-rate loans	High-rate loan volume, in billions	All loan volume, in billions	Percentage high-rate
McAllen-Edinburg-Mission, Texas	17,511	$1.41	$3.61	39.1%
Detroit-Livonia-Dearborn, Mich.	112,183	9.84	30.64	32.1
Miami-Miami Beach-Kendall, Fla.	170,938	29.32	92.78	31.6
Bakersfield, Calif.	53,881	8.10	26.75	30.2
Ocala, Fla.	15,085	1.67	6.21	27.0
Stockton, Calif.	46,447	10.66	40.63	26.2
Cape Coral-Fort Myers, Fla.	52,106	8.50	33.17	25.6
Lewiston-Auburn, Maine	3,843	0.40	1.71	23.8
Las Vegas-Paradise, Nev.	149,892	25.70	109.44	23.4
Tacoma, Wash.	42,335	6.07	27.97	21.7

Source: Home Mortgage Disclosure Act data

Homeowners, however, shouldn't get too worried about the value of their home. Perspective, not panic, is always the first step in assessing the situation. Despite the scary headlines, the vast majority of homeowners are still sitting on decent gains, even if the value of their homes has declined over the past couple of years.

It's important to understand that home values rocketed in the early part of the century in a flukish way. Those kinds of gains won't be seen again anytime soon. Home prices, after the current shakeout ends, are most likely to resume their steady, nearly humdrum appreciation of value.

Also, interest rates remain low and you may be eligible for a refinancing, which is something a shrewd homeowner should always consider. If you are carrying expensive debt, such as credit card debt, refinancing will enable you to substitute cheaper debt for more expensive debt. In such a strategy, you refinance your home and take "cash" out of the house in the form of a new, slightly larger mortgage. The mortgage associated with this cash almost always carries a lower interest rate than credit card and other high-interest-rate debt, making such a debt "swap" rewarding for individuals. The perfect cash-out refinance takes advantage of lower mortgage rates, uses cash to pay down credit card debt and doesn't result in higher monthly payments, because of the lower mortgage rates.

But never take a large risk with your home. Approach any home-related debt with prudence. In times such as these, simply holding on to your house and riding out the current downturn is important. It is a buyer's market, and homes take some time to sell. If you are forced to sell quickly, you may get a really lousy price—and if you haven't had your home very long, there's a good chance that you'll sell at a loss.

If you are struggling with the mortgage and refinancing is not an option, talk to your bank. Although bankers are in a stingy mood, many will talk with you about reworking your mortgage if you are under particular stress. There are many negotiating options, such as paying only interest for a period of time or making partial payments. After all, most banks would prefer to work something out, if possible, and keep you in your home rather than foreclose. They have plenty of empty homes on their books already.

In addition, get creative about extracting more cash from your home. An obvious way is to rent out the basement or a room. Defer putting in that new kitchen, instead putting that money into your investments to build a larger cash cushion to weather the hard times.

Ultimately, if you need to sell, it's important to know that the housing downturn cuts both ways. You may not get the price you once could have, but buying a new place will be cheaper than in the past.

Auto Debt

It's smartest to acquire a car with cash or with as little debt as possible. As we've learned in the past two years, the mounting piles of debt consumers accrue can lead to terrible problems. Many people borrowed too much to buy more home than they needed. They often did similar things when acquiring cars.

If you have a heavy car debt, there are some basic strategies to reduce your debt. The simplest is to sell your car, pay down the debt and get something cheaper. As you will see if you do the research, a used car is most times a better value than a brand-new car. Most brand-new cars lose a chunk of value the moment you drive them off the lot. The new-car smell really isn't worth all that. So-called certified preowned cars are usually the best option. These cars have been inspected and come with a manufacturer's warranty that a used-car lot doesn't usually offer.

At a minimum, your car costs shouldn't be more than 20% of your disposable income. This figure should include your loan payment, insurance, fuel and other vehicle-related expenses. If you're paying more than that, you should take action to reduce your car debt burden.

Student Debt

Many younger folks coming out of college or graduate school face a large student loan burden. Higher education is widely considered a good investment since it equips people to perform better in our fast-moving, constantly changing economy. Still, it's one more form of debt that needs to be dealt with.

Since folks usually face student loan debt while young, cash flow is often a more important consideration than paying down the debt outright. Also, student loan debt generally has a more favorable interest rate than other debt, making it less burdensome. For instance, it's not a shrewd move to pay off student loan debt with a high-interest-rate credit card. Still, as with all debt, it's smart to pay it off as quickly as you reasonably can.

One strategy for dealing with student loan debt is by consolidating it. Most students emerge from college with several loans, each with their own payments. Student loans come in two flavors, private loans from banks and government-backed student loans. Consolidation usually requires you to keep these loans separate to retain your lower interest rates. Also, you can usually consolidate your loans only once.

The best forms of consolidation involve taking advantage of an improving credit score. If your score has improved since you took out the loans, some consolidators will offer you a reduced interest rate, which would reduce your payments.

Another form of consolidation, similar to credit card debt consolidation, bundles your loans and extends the payment period. This reduces your monthly payment, but you end up paying more money over the course of the loan repayment since you're taking more time to pay down the debt. It's not an optimal solution, but sometimes it's a necessary solution as you try to get your financial house in order.

A Last Thought on Debt

Pay it down. As you've read, there are a number of strategies to do that within each debt category. One additional strategy that you should consider is borrowing from yourself to pay down debt. This may sound strange, but at many companies you can borrow money from your 401(k) retirement program. You pay yourself back, with interest, through payroll deductions until the loan is repaid.

There are risks to this approach, of course. If the market takes off while you are in debt to yourself, you won't participate in the rally as fully. Also, if you lose or leave your job, you need to pay yourself back promptly, usually within 60 days. If you took out a big loan and now have no job, that could pose a problem. If you don't pay yourself back, the loan counts as an early withdrawal and you have to pay taxes and penalties on the amount of money owed.

The government may alter rules to permit a one-time tax- and penalty-free withdrawal from your retirement account, but that's still being debated. Without such a change, you should avoid tapping your retirement account directly until you retire. You'll need that money later.

FAQ

Is it ever wise to take on debt?

Yes, but only in two very specific circumstances. One, taking on debt to pay for your college or graduate education makes sense. It's a sound investment in your future. Two, taking on debt, via a mortgage, to buy a home is also logical. In the case of a home, don't buy too much home—make sure you can make the 20% down payment, and don't experiment in exotic mortgage instruments. Keeping it simple is the best way to avoid the mortgage-related calamities that hit so many people before, during and after this financial crisis.

What about borrowing to buy a car?

Many people would say, "No problem." I would argue otherwise. In a time of thrift, such as today, I would try to pay cash for my car. That might mean a big downgrade, but it would also reduce some of the worrisome debt burden so many are facing. If you do feel that you must borrow, follow the 20% guideline outlined above.

Can you really borrow against your 401(k)?

Yes, and I've done it myself. But this should be a last resort. By taking out a loan from yourself, you take money away from your retirement account, reducing its ability to grow. Of course, in a market such as this one, for younger

FAQ

people especially, such concerns are probably front-of-mind.

How many credit cards should I have?

None. Well . . . I'll admit that's not really practical, so let's say one, but make it a card that you have to pay back every month, such as an American Express card. Some places will only take a Visa or MasterCard, in which case you can either use your bank debit card or a special card that you use only for these special circumstances and pay off every month. Credit card debt has caused more problems than nearly any other kind of debt in the U.S. Avoid it.

Should I sell retirement assets to pay down expensive credit card debt?

In the case of 401(k) programs and other programs that are penalized for early withdrawal and have tax advantages, I would say never sell. The penalties will overwhelm any interest rate benefit you get from paying off the credit card debt. You are better off borrowing from your 401(k), thereby avoiding the penalties.

FAQ

What about borrowing from a peer-to-peer lending site to pay down debt?

These are young and untested sites that are best avoided. Let someone else work out the kinks before deciding whether or not to tap them as either a lender or a borrower (though Shakespeare admonishes us to be neither). These sites may become great boons for consumers in a manner similar to how PayPal took off, but it's still too early to tell if they will succeed as PayPal did. Also, borrowing to pay down debt is a bad habit that only the government seems to do over and over again without lacking for lenders. We don't have the government's track record or its ability to raise money, so we shouldn't emulate the government when it comes to debt.

CHECKLIST FOR PAYING DOWN DEBT

1. Establish a monthly budget and find savings that will help reduce or eliminate your debt. A handy strategy is to pretend that gasoline prices remain $4 a gallon, even though they have dropped to $2 a gallon or less in most places. Use the money you would've spent—and were spending earlier in 2008—and apply it to debt reduction.

2. Check your mortgage rate and see if a refinancing will save you money. You can even consider a cash-out refinancing to replace expensive credit card debt with cheaper home-related debt.

3. If your debt is overwhelming and you've tried everything else, consider consolidating your debt to reduce your monthly payment. This should be avoided if possible, because it increases the amount of debt you ultimately pay back. But, it is an option if you need to buy some financial space.

4. Get creative. Renting out a room in your house can help defray expenses and reduce debts. Use public transportation or walk rather than drive everywhere. Thrift comes in many forms and can help you whittle away your debt burden.

EIGHT

ON INVESTMENT STRATEGY

NOW THAT YOU KNOW what's safe and you have some strategies to lower your debt, it's time to think about investing again. In the end, money in the mattress will not grow. Indeed, inflation chips away at inactive cash like so many drips from the faucet. It might feel strange to think about investing and building your nest egg when the world of finance has become frighteningly difficult to figure out. But the nation has faced difficult times in the past and will get through them again, no matter how glum the headlines appear.

Before delving into investment strategies, let's get some perspective on the current environment. Several important investors have stepped in to buy shares since the financial panic intensified last September. Most notably, Warren Buffett, the Sage of Omaha and arguably the best investor alive, grabbed stakes in Wall Street giant Goldman Sachs and industrial conglomerate General Electric. Buffett gets preferred treatment in such deals, so it's impossible to mimic his exact moves. But he invested in two firms with enormous financial exposure, which means he believed these firms would survive. People forget that General Electric, while making jet engines and turbines, also has a very large financial business. Buffett's endorsement is worth noting. He, of course, is a long-term player, not a white-knuckle trader. That's another reason to take solace in his approach.

Also, it's important to note that we've had panics before. The most recent came when the dot-com bubble crashed in the early part of the decade. This debacle hit the entire market, but the technology market was especially affected. The Nasdaq Composite Index remains well below the highs seen at the peak of the Internet mania, but the broader market recovered before heading lower this past year. The prolonged slump in Internet stocks is a prime example of why investors must be diversified to have the best chance at good, risk-adjusted returns.

How you save and invest depends a great deal on your personal situation. There are some broad-based rules that can help anybody devise a sound personal finance strategy. But whether you are young or old has a bearing on what kind of risk you should take and what kind of tactics you should employ.

First we'll cover the basic rules of the road that any investor should heed. Then we'll take three snapshots to illustrate how young people, middle-aged folks and those close to or in retirement should deal with the new landscape.

WARREN BUFFETT

Warren Buffett has earned a reputation as the best investor in the world. Through Berkshire Hathaway, the company he runs, he has amassed an enormous fortune for himself and his investors and acquired many well-known companies such as Dairy Queen and Geico.

At its heart, Berkshire Hathaway is an insurance company. His insurance units' premiums provide Mr. Buffett with a "float" of cash that he has used to drive his investments. He is a noted "value" investor, looking for underpriced assets and acquiring them, believing that the assets will rise to reach their true value. Value investors are considered conservative and usually hold their investments for a long period of time. Mr. Buffett has himself held large stakes in Coca-Cola, the Washington Post Co. and Wells Fargo for some time.

Living in Omaha, Neb., Mr. Buffett has crafted a folksy image that belies his obvious investment acumen. He usually drives himself, has a modest office space decorated with various mementos and has chided companies for paying executives exorbitant compensation.

His annual letters to shareholders are cleverly written and contain a combination of corporate reporting, witty remarks and commentary about the economy. He has long warned about the dangers of derivatives, and his foresight in that area helped him avoid the messes that have befallen other companies.

He also famously said he didn't get the technology stock boom in the late 1990s, so he avoided it. For a time, this led to much criticism, but, as so often has been the case, Mr. Buffett came out of the bubble era smelling like a rose.

Given his enormous resources and impressive track record, many people look to Mr. Buffett when things grow dire. He has dabbled in companies involved in the financial crisis, notably Goldman Sachs and General Electric, but he has mostly remained on the sidelines. His difficulties in "rescuing" Salomon Brothers in the early 1990s may have made him leery of diving in too deeply during the current financial crisis. (Salomon eventually became part of what is Citigroup today.)

Mr. Buffett burnished his iconic status when he pledged to give nearly all of his accumulated wealth to the Bill & Melinda Gates Foundation upon his death.

The Basics

Every investor needs to start somewhere. Saving money is the first order of the day. There's an old adage: Pay yourself first. This applies whether you are just out of college or fitting out for another game of golf. Younger folks should focus more squarely on getting rid of debt, but even setting aside a small amount of money will build a habit of savings and thrift that will translate into a better investment position when you start to make more money.

Diversification is vital. That means thinking beyond the stock market. An investor, depending on his or her short-term needs and long-term responsibilities, should have a mix of stocks, bonds, commodities and real estate. Ideally, you should diversify within each of those baskets as well. Oftentimes, folks end up investing too heavily in a single sector. Many people overdosed on technology during the dot-com bubble. The same occurred when the real estate mania led people to overborrow in a bid to add more homes to their portfolios. Too many eggs in one basket spell trouble when the basket drops. Best to have several baskets with fewer eggs in each one.

An investor must also have patience. Individuals have historically sold heaviest at market bottoms and purchased stocks when they have become too dear. Having a set strategy that is diversified and focused on your goals provides resistance to panic. That doesn't mean to ignore your holdings. As some investments rise in value, you may need to rebalance your position in order to stick to the game plan you devised. Rebalancing ensures that you sell winners and, ideally, invest in those that are about to win. This practice also reduces the prospect that you will get caught in a mania and its usually bad aftermath. When technology shares soared in the late 1990s, many investors inadvertently became overexposed to that sector by simply doing nothing. Eventually, simply by holding technology stocks, that sector became an overly dominant part of an investor's portfolio. With stock investing, especially in new markets, your strategy should not be to buy and hold forever but rather to buy, hold and beware.

Always take advantage of free money. Many companies offer matching money for investments in your 401(k) program. Typically this match is dollar for dollar or some percentage of each

PENSIONS AND 401(K)S

Retirement investment plans have a relatively short history and have evolved into a bifurcated system containing defined-benefit plans, better known as pensions, and defined-contribution plans, better known as 401(k) or 403(b) plans.

Pension plans became popular during World War II when companies sought to compensate employees during a period of wage freezes and other restrictions. Under a pension plan, the company accrues money and invests it on behalf of its workers. Over time, the workers are "vested" into the plan and then upon retirement receive a monthly payment, often in perpetuity.

These plans made a lot of sense when people generally went to work at a company for most of their life and didn't live as long as they do now. People who moved jobs frequently would usually not work at one place long enough to become "vested" in the pension plan and would therefore not receive payments upon retirement.

Defined-contribution plans, mostly 401(k)s, came into existence in 1980 after Congress passed laws that provided tax benefits to these kinds of retirement accounts. Employees contribute pretax income to their 401(k) and use the funds in the 401(k) to invest in an array of instruments such as mutual funds and stocks. At 59½ years of age, investors can start withdrawing funds from their 401(k) without penalty. Taxes are paid on the funds withdrawn.

These plans are portable in the sense that an employee can keep the funds if he or she switches jobs.

Most companies today provide 401(k) plans, leaving the retirement burden on the employee. Some companies and many government institutions still maintain pension plans, but the tide is definitely moving in the other direction, primarily because management of a 401(k) plan is less costly than providing a pension plan.

dollar you invest, capped annually. Inexplicably, many employees do not take advantage of this free money or neglect their retirement program altogether. Don't make that mistake.

Don't pay attention to the talking heads on television. They are traders, not investors, and they often bark loudly and wrong and at the most inopportune moment. If economists have called ten of the last three recessions, investment barkers have called three hundred of the last two market bottoms. There's entertainment value in some of the barking, but it's best ignored. Spend more time with your family or a good book; that's probably a wiser investment.

Last, since every circumstance is unique, consider talking to a financial adviser. While this book contains basic, sensible ideas about how to shape your personal finance strategy, investment in more detailed and tailored advice is a wise idea. Fee-based certified financial planners are the best. They are focused on giving you advice, not on selling you products. The best way to find these planners is by asking friends. If that doesn't work, you can do an Internet search for planners in your area.

Before agreeing to hire a planner, here are some key issues you should address. The planner should be willing to meet you in person before you actually hire him or her. The planner should be willing to respond to emails and phone calls quickly. Also, you should discuss the planner's financial philosophy to ensure a good fit. Lastly, inquire after the planner's past successes and difficulties. Candor is often a good sign. Never forget that the planner is working for you; he or she should behave that way.

A Word on Real Estate

After a couple of years of falling home prices, homeowners are understandably nervous about how they can protect what for most is their biggest asset.

For investors in stocks and bonds, successful strategies to combat the ups and downs of the marketplace are fairly straightforward. Have a diversified portfolio to balance risk, be disciplined about consistently saving money and don't chase returns or the latest fad.

Homeowners face a trickier landscape. Diversification in real estate isn't really possible. Owning ten homes, besides being very expensive, just multiplies the trouble in a falling market. Also, buying and selling homes isn't as easy as buying and selling mutual funds or shares.

But there are steps you as a homeowner can take that can help you ride out the housing storm.

For starters, don't get too addled about the value of your home. Perspective, not panic, is always the first step in assessing the situation. Despite the scary headlines, the vast majority of homeowners are still sitting on decent gains, even if the value of their home has declined over the past couple of years.

Still, don't forget that for all the ballyhoo of the early 2000s, return on residential real estate has trailed stocks over time. According to research by the Yale economist Robert Shiller, the average historic return on homes has been about 3% a year, roughly on par with inflation. Stocks, on average, have historically performed more than twice as well. These calculations focus on the top-line gains—the purchase and sale prices. Whereas shares don't require much maintenance, a home is an entirely different matter. A new roof, property taxes, the cost of your mortgage, various repairs and improvements all chip away at the investment value of a home.

Still, given the weak housing market, hunting for ways to protect the value of your home—or to ameliorate your losses—is wise. It might be tempting to consider house-specific solutions, but there really aren't any that make sense for most folks.

For instance, the Chicago Mercantile Exchange trades indexes that track home prices in 10 cities and nationwide that can be used to hedge against home price declines. But these instruments are complex, expensive and aimed primarily at big players, such as home builders, who are looking for ways to hedge against the risks associated with hundreds of homes as opposed to a single residence.

Other home-specific strategies involve exotic maneuvers such as shorting bonds or stocks that correlate with housing prices. Again, this entails a high level of risk and is best left to the professionals.

But there are simpler ways to address your housing concerns. For starters, rather than worrying about your home, focus on the rest of your portfolio as an overall hedge against falling home prices. This would require steering clear of real estate–oriented stocks such as real estate investment trusts, home builders, mortgage companies and home-improvement stores. You should make sure the rest of your portfolio is well diversified, and if you are more risk-averse because of your fragile home asset, consider adding to your fixed-income assets.

You should also examine your debt, especially your mortgage. Interest rates remain low, and you may be eligible for a refinancing, which is something a shrewd homeowner should always consider. If you are carrying expensive debt, such as credit card debt, refinancing enables you to swap cheaper debt for more expensive debt.

In times such as these, simply holding on to your house and riding out the current downturn is important. It is a buyer's market, and homes take some time to sell. If you are forced to sell quickly, you may get a really lousy price, and if you haven't held your home very long, there's a good chance that you'll sell at a loss.

Advice for Young People Just Starting Out

This is a time when you should not be overly worried about the stock market, especially as it relates to retirement planning. Because of your youth, you can take more risks. That's simply a function of time. Through the decades, investments in stocks have performed better than those in any other asset, including homes. Stocks have typically returned close to 8% annually over time, more than double real estate's long-term appreciation rate, though there can be extended troughs, as we've seen in the past.

In your 401(k) program, you should be fully invested in the stock market with a dollop of overseas holdings. The tumult of recent months has made stocks extraordinarily cheap on a valuation basis, and since you have decades to wait before retirement, you should take full advantage of that reality. It might take some time for things to recover, but you have that time. If you start young, even with small amounts, the effects of compounding will help your nest egg grow.

This is also a time to build the discipline and habits that will serve you in later life. Save when you can, pay down debt aggressively and keep things sensible. In the coming time of thrift, budgets will become sexier than a fancy dinner or a trip to Vegas. By being smart now, you will pave the way for a more successful, enriching life down the road. You have loads of the most valuable commodity around: time. Don't waste it.

In terms of near-term needs, such as graduate school or starting a family, the stock market may not be your friend. It is, after all, a risky place to invest. With risk comes return, but it's never certain when and how much that return will be. If you do decide to save for graduate school through investing, you can set up your own 529 plan. This type of plan, named for its reference in the tax code, allows you to make tax-advantaged investments in stocks or bonds. Usually people set up such a plan to save for their children's college, which is a worthy goal. But you can also apply the account to your own educational spending.

Other near-term investment strategies could include buying municipal bonds or certificates of deposit. Municipal bonds pay a bit better than CDs and can be tax-free. But be careful about what muni bonds you acquire. Many towns and states will face stiff economic headwinds as the economy works through the downturn, and some muni bonds could find themselves at risk. The ratings agencies provide some guidance here, so check on the ratings of bonds before making a purchase.

Certificates of deposit have modestly outsized interest rates right now, primarily because banks are eager for cash deposits. You can get 3.5% for a one-year CD at some banks. If you have a large slug of cash, a so-called jumbo CD can pay even a bit more. CDs aren't exotic, and they are insured by the FDIC up to $250,000, so they are very safe investments.

For near-term needs, it is best to put together a mixture of safe investments, such as CDs, Treasury bonds or muni bonds, and some exposure to the stock market. A good rule of thumb, especially in the treacherous environment we presently are in, is not to put more than 50% of your near-term investment cash into the stock market. Even that figure might be aggressive.

At this age real estate is a huge investment. Since the end of the real estate bubble, real estate has become relatively cheap in many markets. The challenge is securing the financing to acquire real estate. Don't look at real estate as a short-term investment. It's not clear how long the overhang on real estate could last, but it's likely to be some time. Previous bubbles in other sectors and places—the Internet, Japan, Thoroughbred horses—have led to a sustained period of weakness in the aftermath. Homes could see a similar trajectory.

Therefore, think about real estate based on your needs. Renting might be a better option if you are thinking of moving sometime soon or starting a family. If you do want to acquire a house, think of two things. First, you should have the 20% of the purchase price in cash to make a down payment. This gives you a slug of equity right away and disciplines you into not buying too much home. Second, consider your needs and make sure you are acquiring the house for sensible lifestyle reasons. This is the old-fashioned way of thinking about a home, and it is likely to prevail once again. Over time, your home may or may not return you much money. But it is a place where you can live, and there's something to be said for that.

How you start your life in the working world often has an outsized impact on how you will retire from that stage of your life. Paying down debt, saving money, investing sensibly and having a sound personal finance approach will pay dividends.

Advice for Those in the Middle of Life

You are caught betwixt and between. No longer burdened with the debts and low income of your youth nor facing the prospect of retirement, the demands on you have blossomed. You may have a family, own a home, be saving for retirement and your kids' college and also trying to best navigate the tricky economy and threatening job environment. With so much happening, making a plan is especially important.

First, your retirement account. You still have a couple of decades before you retire and face long, blissful years after that. You shouldn't get too worried about the stock market's decline, but you should be examining your holdings, ensuring that they are properly diversified. In addition, with retirement no longer a crazy and distant notion but actually starting to come into focus, you should start increasing your safer, fixed-income holdings. A good rule of thumb is to subtract the age of the head of the household from 110 to determine the amount of appropriate exposure to the stock market. Thus, at the age of 40, you should have 70% of your retirement assets in stocks and the remainder of those assets in safer, fixed-income investments such as Treasury Inflation-Protected Securities (TIPS), which are priced to eliminate or diminish inflation risk over time.

With the stock market down so sharply, moving those holdings into safer investments doesn't make a lot of sense. Instead, you should focus on putting new 401(k) contributions into these assets in order to reshape the balance of your portfolio. It is still a good time to take risk, since you still have a number of years before retirement, but it also makes sense to start edging toward a more prudent approach.

Savings for your children's college education depends a bit on how old the kids are. Some may be right about to enter college. The best way to save for college is through a 529 plan, which can be a mixture of stocks and bonds. Each state sets up its own plans, and you can invest in any state's plan. Each has its own advantages that you need to examine for your own needs.

Think about the 529 plan as similar to your retirement account, with the start of college as the equivalent of retirement. You should be aggressive, with a large exposure to stocks and international investments, early in the plan and steadily shift the plan to a more prudent footing as the college years approach. You don't want to lose a large chunk of the plan's holdings because of a stock market dive on the eve of matriculation.

Real estate is an interesting issue at this stage. Your home value has likely declined, but so have other home values around you. Values are present, and you still will want the use of a good home for at least another 20 years. If you have paid down much of your mortgage and don't have the need for immediate cash, now might be a good time to test the market. If you don't have to sell, you can wait a good amount of time to see if someone will meet the price that you desire. On the other side, there are many eager and sometimes desperate sellers, making this a buyer's market. You can strike an excellent deal and improve your home situation. Of course, don't get greedy. Make sure you have the cash to make the 20% down payment, and don't raid the kids' college fund or your retirement to make the deal happen. Homes, as we've noted, are not likely to be a great investment, even in the long term.

Advice for Those Near or at Retirement

This has to be a very confounding and frustrating time for many at or near retirement. Large chunks of investments have evaporated. Retirement dates are being pushed back, and some retirees are returning to work. After many years of building a retirement nest egg, things have suddenly gone awry.

Folks in this bracket face special, sharp challenges. Many of the old bromides don't apply so well. Safe investments, which retirees should focus on, are paying rock-bottom interest rates. Homes, usually a store of wealth, have lost ground. And the job market isn't exactly booming for people of any age.

Of course, many people in this stage of their life are in terrific shape. They have no debt, their home is owned free and clear and though the stock market has hit hard, it hasn't hit too badly. Travel, tennis and thumbing through a good book are foremost on your mind. I say a hearty congratulations to you!

If only everyone had it so well. But if your current situation is looking grimmer, don't despair. There are some strategies that can help you weather the storm.

People are living much longer. Retirement at 65 can mean a couple of decades or more ahead before being called home. That means that you still have time for the stock market to recover if you've invested heavily there. Folks at this stage in their lives shouldn't be too deep into the stock market, but saying that today feels like yapping about horses well out of the barn. You are where you are. Selling your stocks now at a loss may not be the shrewdest response to the current situation. Indeed, the government may enact changes in basic retirement programs to make it possible to keep your money in the market rather than have to make minimum required withdrawals, usually in the 3–4% range, depending on your circumstances, beginning at age 70. If so, you should take advantage of this rule change while the market is down.

Even though home values have dropped, most retirees'

homes still retain a lot of equity. You can downsize your home and move into something smaller, pocketing the difference and putting that into investments. You could also take out a reverse mortgage, which would permit you to stay in the home while extracting the equity value in the home over time. This is not a great strategy right now for two reasons. One, it's expensive, so looking for other ways to raise cash first, including an outright sale, is preferable. Two, with home values shaky, there's a chance that your home may not have enough value to pay back the reverse mortgage when you leave the home behind. That would mean potentially saddling your estate with a good-sized debt.

Social Security payments will also come in handy, more for some than for others. Delaying the start of your payments until you can receive the highest monthly payment (usually starting around 67 years of age) is prudent, if you are able to do so.

If you have some cash because of a home sale or retirement income or from the sale of other assets or stocks, what is the right deployment strategy? You should employ a mix of opportunism and prudence, erring toward the side of keeping the money you've saved and earned over the course of a lifetime. If you already have stock exposure, as mentioned above, there's little reason to add to it. You might analyze the mix of your holdings to make sure your portfolio is well diversified and not overly speculative. If you are heavily or entirely invested in stocks, you should move some of that money out of the market gradually and place it in safer investments, such as bonds or certificates of deposit. Investment advisers recommend that you diminish your exposure to the stock market over the course of your life, moving increasingly into safer, fixed-income investments as you get older. Based on our earlier life cycle calculation (head of household age subtracted from 110), at age 70, you should have about 40% in stocks and the remainder of your assets in safer, fixed-income securities. For most people in this age range, the stock market swoon has probably reoriented your stock exposure to a much smaller slice of your portfolio.

There are several strategies to use in the fixed-income space. A popular one is "laddering" municipal bonds or Treasury bonds. If you want to reach for a little bit more yield, you can use this strategy with corporate bonds as well. All bonds are rated, and since retirees should focus on capital preservation, you should invest in only highly rated bonds. If a corporate bond has a surprisingly high interest rate, that just means that investors are concerned that the company will default on its bond debts. You don't want to take that kind of risk.

"Laddering" means buying bonds in ever-lengthening durations. You purchase one-year, two-year, three-year bonds and so forth up to a ten-year bond. As the one-year bond comes due, you purchase another ten-year bond to keep the ladder in place. This reduces the risk that you will overload on overly low bond yields and provides a steady stream of income. It is considered a safe approach, but it also doesn't pay very high yields since the Federal Reserve took short-term interest rates down to nearly 0% in late 2008 and short-term government bonds are paying extremely low interest rates.

You can also use laddering on certificates of deposit, and

some CDs are paying a bit higher rate these days so banks can attract more capital. But again, these are not the greatest rates in the land for the same reasons that bonds aren't paying very high rates.

If you have time and the stomach for the risk, you could look at purchasing some individual stocks. Dividend-paying stocks make the most sense because this strategy will ensure some income even if the market continues to struggle. But be careful of overly generous dividend yields. Dividend yields average about 3% among Standard & Poor's 500-stock index companies. Anything closer to 8% or 10% could indicate a dividend in trouble. The yield is calculated by taking the annual yield and dividing it into the value of the stock. The yield therefore mushrooms when the stock price dives. More often than not, a large yield presages a cut in dividend payments. Don't forget: if it looks too good to be true, it usually is.

Last, if all of your strategies leave you short of cash, you can try to go back to work. Traditional employment may be tough to find, but many retirees have set up businesses online. My retired father, for instance, sells antique glass on eBay. Others have found ways to turn a hobby, such as quilt making, into a profession and develop sales channels online. Going back to work after retiring may sound like a drag, but if you can exploit your hobbies, skills and accumulated knowledge in a creative way, you might find it more fun than the work you did before hanging up your boots.

FAQ

Why a fee-only financial planner?

For starters, everyone's financial situation is singular. You can gather basics and broad-based advice from various sources, including this book. But to get into the nitty-gritty, it makes sense to fork over a few bucks to a certified financial planner. Be sure to do due diligence first. Ask friends for leads, and when you find some prospective planners, be sure to ask them some hard questions. What's their track record? Have them name some successes as well as a failure. Ask them if they will explain their processes and philosophy before taking your fee. If they won't, keep on looking. Ask them how they interact with clients after an initial meeting. Do they prefer email or phone calls? How quickly do they usually respond? If the planner is uncomfortable with this kind of grilling, he or she is not the right planner for you.

Should I think differently about the stock market after the financial crisis?

In some ways, yes. Many people became too sanguine about the stock market, treating it more like a bank than the risky place it actually is. It will remain a good long-term place for long-term investments. But if you need money in the short term, safer investments such as certificates of deposit and highly rated municipal bonds present

FAQ

a better option. Also, when investing in the stock market, low-cost index funds make more sense than trying to arrange a diversified portfolio of actively managed funds. Index funds save you money and give you diversification. Over a long period of time, savings on fees can add up significantly. Also, most actively managed funds underperform index funds over time.

Should I consider "life-cycle" funds that adjust over time to take on less risk as I get older?
In some circumstances, yes. If you don't want to spend a lot of time managing your accounts, this approach makes sense. It is, however, more expensive, in terms of fees, than managing the life-cycle realities on your own. As you grow older, you should reduce your exposure to stocks and increase your exposure to safer, fixed-income investments.

What about commodities?
Many investment advisers believe that a small exposure to commodities, usually about 5% of your overall portfolio, should go into commodities. This provides a hedge against inflation and diversifies your portfolio mix. Commodities are incredibly volatile—note how oil prices dropped from $147 a barrel to $41 a barrel in just a few months. A lot of

FAQ

people don't have the stomach for that kind of risk. If so, you'll be fine focusing on broad-based index funds to achieve proper diversification.

Should I invest in real estate?

Only for a place to live. Real estate, barring the crazy years of the real estate bubble, has historically been a humdrum asset, returning about 3% a year, or the rate of inflation, whereas stocks have returned about 6% to 8% over time. When buying a home, make sure you have enough for a 20% down payment and sufficient resources to cover the mortgage payments. Enjoy your home as it was meant to be enjoyed—as a place to live and raise your family in.

INVESTMENT CHECKLIST

1. Talk to a fee-only financial adviser. Every person's investment situation is unique, and getting some professional guidance is a good first step. A fee-only adviser, unlike an adviser who is paid to sell you certain products, is not beholden to anyone but you.

2. Establish a diversification strategy that will help you build assets while reducing risk. Risk, of course, can't be eliminated, but diversification helps diminish the danger.

3. Focus on low-fee investments that provide diversity, such as stock index mutual funds. Most actively managed mutual funds historically underperform the market on average, and they have higher fees. Over the life of building an investment nest egg, small fees can add up, so be mindful of what you spend in fees.

4. Don't take on too much risk. The stock market is risky, as we've all learned. Over the long haul, it does well, but in the short term stocks can create a lot of heartburn. Make sure that you have the right risk profile to suit your situation. Again, a fee-only adviser can help you understand your own risk tolerance.

5. Your home should be your home. Make sure it is affordable, and don't view it as the road to riches. It will store value at about the rate of inflation, but unlike in the recent past, a home is not going to sharply rise in value. It's easier to enjoy your home when it is not an enormous economic burden, so don't buy more home than you can afford.

EPILOGUE

THE FINANCIAL CRISIS OF 2008, like many panics before it, actually started well before it dominated the headlines. Seeds sowed more than a decade beforehand and the steady rise of irrational confidence in complex market mechanisms eventually ended in cataclysmic fashion. Banks collapsed, and entire countries faced economic hardship of a severe nature. Individuals collectively lost trillions of dollars in savings. Home values fell, and foreclosures soared. For a few weeks at the height of the panic, it appeared that the center might not hold. The entire system hung precariously in the balance.

Most observers believe the worst of the crisis is behind us, but it's difficult to say for certain. For instance, regulators believed the bullet had been dodged in early September, only to see Lehman, Merrill and AIG blow up two weeks later. Similarly, a calm hovered over the markets in mid-October, but less than one month later Citigroup needed a huge government lifeline. Like a patient who has whipped cancer, the prospect of the nightmare's return will persist for some time.

Meantime, as the system has lurched from one catastrophe to another, the real economy has steadily weakened. Growth has slowed sharply, unemployment has risen and home values in many parts of the country continue to drop. Most economists believe the global economy will shrink throughout 2009, with some calling for a recovery toward the end of the year. More bankruptcies, nationalizations and rescues could be ahead of us. Other companies survive in zombie status—walking, dazed and financially extremely fragile or only just better than broken. Consumer confidence is at an all-time low, and spending has dropped dramatically. It's not a pretty picture.

But what many people forget is that what's so remarkable about the democratic capitalistic system is its resilience. Panics have come and gone, but the system has always found ways to fix itself and bounce back. There's no question that the task ahead of us all is enormous, and the government, companies and individuals will all have a role to play in fixing what has gone awry. A number of people have lost their jobs, and more will lose theirs in the months ahead. Though a job loss is devastating, it is also an opportunity for reinvention. If you keep your job, think about helping others who are less fortunate. There's a chance for volunteerism, community spirit and our better angels, perhaps hiding underground during boom times, to rise once again.

How Past Crises Were Handled

The Panic of 1792: The federal government added about $18 million to its domestic debt of $65 million after it took on states' debts from the Revolutionary War. Speculators swarmed to the securities, but when the bubble burst rapidly, Treasury Secretary Alexander Hamilton had a bold solution: borrow from the banks to buy the troubled bonds, boosting their market price.

The Panic of 1907: Amid a run on banks and trusts which had made loans for a failed attempt to corner the market on stock in a copper company, confidence in other financial institutions waned rapidly. Banking magnate J. P. Morgan gathered New York's bankers at his home, where they worked through the night until he persuaded them to form a joint pool of capital to pay depositors at banks under threat.

The Depression: The Home Owners' Loan Corp. created by President Roosevelt and Congress bought defaulted mortgages from banks, refinancing them at lower rates for fixed, 15-year terms, to about 1 million homeowners as homeowners floundered in the wake of the stock market crash. With no secondary market for securitized mortgages, the agency had to hold the mortgages for their full terms.

Savings and Loan crisis: From 1986 to 1995, about half of the country's 3,234 savings and loans closed up shop, following a failed expansion into commercial real-estate lending. Congress responded by creating the Resolution Trust Corp., to make depositors whole and clean up the industry, to the tune of at least $124 billion.

Source: staff reports

More prosaically, as in the Crash of 1929 and the Great Depression that followed, new rules will be written to govern our system and large chances will be taken as the government tries to spur a return to growth. Sometimes the government will get it wrong, but even former Federal Reserve Chairman Alan Greenspan—long an opponent of most financial regulation— argues that some new regulation is necessary for the proper functioning of our complex, high-tech marketplace.

The new administration will have a key role to play in the recovery. Large infrastructure investments and other public spending are expected. Tax hikes, even on the rich, may not reach center stage until the economy starts to expand again.

The timing of the crisis, in a way, is fortuitous. With the re-election campaign four years away, the Obama team has time to act boldly to solve problems outside the glare of election-year politicking. And President Obama has selected a top-rate economic team to tackle the challenges ahead. Timothy Geithner, formerly the head of the New York Federal Reserve Bank, will be the Treasury secretary. Former Clinton Treasury Secretary Lawrence Summers will work on economics from the White House. And former Fed chief Paul Volcker, widely credited with slaying inflation in the early 1980s, will also have a role to play on the Obama economic team. This core team has received nods of approval across the political spectrum. They will propose large spending and stimulus programs to try to revive the economy, and they will also write the new rules that will augment the governance of our financial system.

It's important to note that there's no shortage of regulation already. From the Securities and Exchange Commission to states' attorneys general to newer wrinkles such as the massive Sarbanes-Oxley corporate regulatory reform acts, there are plentiful overseers and many rules. Still, despite the panoply of rules, it's clear that the system didn't work as intended. I hope that the government takes great care as it writes new rules in the wake of the financial crisis. Financial innovation has played a huge role in driving the American economy, and strangling innovation would be in error. Still, it's important to have workable rules to ensure we have the best chance of a properly running marketplace and economy.

In the end, regulations and laws can't stop what leads to panics: greed and overconfidence. These traits will always be with us to varying degrees. The key is making sure the playing field is well understood by all of us affected by it and that the rule book is clear and enforceable. Mistakes and corruption will happen. The system needs to have mechanisms that suss them out before they become endemic and potentially catastrophic.

For each of us, it is important to learn our own lessons. Thrift has to make a comeback. Prudence and planning in terms of our investments, whether they be stocks or a home, will help us survive chaos. We can't live on borrowed time or thrive indefinitely on borrowed money.

Forecasters have a wide range of expectations for the coming months and years. Most of them are pretty pessimistic, with some forecasting a recession that will top anything we've seen since the Great Depression. Others are more charitable and argue that the downturn will feel like the one we experienced in the early 1980s. That recession included short-term interest rates of nearly 20% and an unemployment rate of 10.8%. It snuffed out the terrible inflation of the 1970s, but at no small cost.

Over the past 30 years, downturns have turned steadily shallower and shorter. Companies have managed inventories and resources more shrewdly, utilizing technology to greatly im-

Big Days
Ten biggest percentage gains in the Dow Jones Industrial Average*

Date	Close	Point change	Percentage change
March 15, 1933	62.10	8.26	15.34%
Oct. 6, 1931	99.34	12.86	14.87
Oct. 30, 1929	258.47	28.40	12.34
Sept. 21, 1932	75.16	7.67	11.36
Oct. 13, 2008	9387.61	936.42	11.08
Oct. 21, 1987	2027.85	186.84	10.15
Aug. 3, 1932	58.22	5.06	9.52
Feb. 11, 1932	78.60	6.80	9.47
Nov. 14, 1929	217.28	18.59	9.36
Dec. 18, 1931	80.69	6.90	9.35

*Through Oct. 13, 2008   Source: Dow Jones Indexes

prove their nimbleness. Individuals have proved resilient as well, retraining, switching jobs and starting small businesses. Most of the hiring done in the U.S. each year is not by large automakers or computer firms but by small businesses. The Small Business Administration and state programs aimed at small business help entrepreneurs get off the ground. As the U.S. economy continues to evolve, the small-business engine will only become more important.

This downturn may prove more resistant to the previous patterns. For a start, home values usually fall after unemployment rises, since home ownership is usually a function of getting a steady paycheck to pay off the mortgage. But the home market declined even before jobs began to disappear. That means that the home market isn't likely to rebound anytime soon.

Problems that plagued the financial markets, especially the credit crunch, spread to all other parts of the economy. Weak players, such as Circuit City in the electronics sector, filed for bankruptcy. The U.S. automakers faced a perilous situation, with millions of jobs at stake. Even so-called healthy companies, such as General Electric, couldn't find short-term loans at certain moments in the crunch, making their cost of business more expensive and limiting their ability to expand and hire.

And consumers have changed their view of money. No longer carefree, they are fearful of the future. Spending is declining, savings are rising. The great deleveraging is taking place at home, too. This is the piece of the puzzle that will be toughest to solve. Consumers account for two-thirds of economic activity in the U.S. If the U.S. consumer is newly and persistently thrifty, that will make the downturn longer and deeper.

Ultimately, getting our personal and corporate financial health back in order is a good thing. The nation has faced steep challenges before and come through them. The long gas lines and high inflation of the 1970s gave way to the booming 1980s and 1990s. Depression and world war gave way to the lucrative 1950s. Also, we as a nation learn from past nightmares. The bank runs of the 1930s led to bank deposit insurance. Impoverished retirees living in squalor made the case for a social security system. Our ability to learn, adapt and come back is one reason that all the breathless talk about the Great Depression is misplaced. Though the situation is challenging, the prospect of sprawling shantytowns and an emptied-out dust bowl are vanishingly small.

We've faced challenges like this before, and I'm optimistic that we will come through this period renewed and reinvigorated. Improved technology has made companies quicker to adapt to changing circumstances. The creative energy of the global economy, especially in Asia, will help fuel a rebound. Moreover, hundreds of millions of people in places like India and Brazil will continue to emerge from poverty and become consumers. All of these things will combine to help the economy rebound. So, don't expect long soup lines and tattered men selling apples from a bucket. The references to the Great Depression are hyperbolic and the product more of reduced memories than of reality.

When everyone on Wall Street believes one thing, usually its opposite is true. Right now, everyone on Wall Street expects a brutally long recession. This is probably because so many workers on Wall Street are watching their jobs disappear. Their pessimism is perhaps augmented by the fact that most in the news business who are writing about the ailing economy and flailing financial system are watching their own jobs disappear with increased frequency. Rather than the long and enduring downturn anticipated by the glum-faced Wall Streeters, look for a more Hobbesian recession: nasty, brutish and short.

ACKNOWLEDGMENTS

In October 2008, with the financial crisis in full bloom, my friend Roe D'Angelo, the director of books and special projects at *The Wall Street Journal*, asked if I'd be interested in writing a book about what had gone amiss and how people should deal with it. It sounded like a great idea, given how many people were asking me those exact questions everyday. Once we decided to do the book, Roe played an elemental role in helping me navigate the process, and I'm very grateful to her.

I'd like to thank my colleagues at FiLife.com who helped with ideas. And I'd like to thank the people at *The Wall Street Journal* and Collins who worked incredibly hard under very tight deadlines to get this book out as quickly as possible. At the *Journal*, I'd like to thank those who helped Roe get things done. Erik Brynildsen, a graphic artist, did terrific work generating art for the book and customized the layout over his Thanksgiving break. Marshall Crook, a news assistant, helped keep things on track. Karen Pensiero, a *Journal* assistant managing editor, vetted the manuscript over a single weekend to ensure it met the paper's high standards. And Dona Wong, the *Journal*'s graphics director, helped corral additional help for the book's artwork.

At the Online Journal, Almar Latour, Nikki Waller and others helped build the online components for the book, including video and interactive graphics.

I would also like to thank Ann Sarnoff, a Dow Jones executive and board member at FiLife, and Shana Fisher, another FiLife board member and an IAC executive, both of whom supported the idea from the beginning. I'd also like to thank Alan Murray, a FiLife board member and *Journal* executive editor for online and books.

Among others at the *Journal*, editors David Crook and Karen Damato helped me flesh out ideas, some of which became columns for the Sunday *Wall Street Journal*. Larry Rout and John Leger also helped me think through individual investor psychology.

At Collins, Sarah Rainone did excellent work as my editor. She had good insights on style, flow and structure. The book writing and editing timeline was so tight that we didn't actually meet until the book headed off to be published, despite working just a couple of miles apart. I'd also like to thank Ben Steinberg, who was instrumental. Many thanks to Leah Carlson Stanisic, Nikki Cutler, Diane Aronson, and Monica Hopkins, in production, and Lynn Anderson for copyediting. Thank you to Nina Brown and Richard Ljoenes for the cover, and to Angie Lee for marketing, Doug Jones for sales, and Larry Hughes for publicity. And I'd also like to thank Steve Ross and Hollis Heimbouch for coming up with and approaching Roe D'Angelo with the idea.

Others outside of Dow Jones and Collins provided excellent ideas. I am thankful for Jim Hyatt, a former boss of mine, who peppered me with suggestions. Jerry Colonna, a former colleague, helped calm me down when it seemed an impossible task to complete the book on time. And my family also had ideas that proved very helpful.

With an army of support, I avoided some dreadful errors, for which I am thankful. Any miscues are certainly my own.

Finally, I want to thank my wife, Monica. We got married in the summer of 2008 and she probably didn't expect her new husband to be locked away writing a book not long thereafter. She provided excellent support and wisdom as I hammered away at my laptop for hours on end, and I am grateful for her love and patience.